Rags *for* Pennies

Best Wishes

Dave x

*This book is in memory of my
lifelong friend Trevor Kendall*

Rags *for* Pennies

Growing Up in Post-War
Stechford, Birmingham

David A. Prosser

BREWIN BOOKS

BREWIN BOOKS
19 Enfield Ind. Estate,
Redditch,
Worcestershire,
B97 6BY
www.brewinbooks.com

Published by Brewin Books 2022

A CIP catalogue record for this book is
available from the British Library.

ISBN: 978-1-85858-749-3

Printed and bound in Great Britain
by Halstan & Co. Ltd.

CONTENTS

	Acknowledgements	ix
	About the Author	xi
	List of Photos and Illustrations	xiii
	Your Life	xv
	Introduction	xvii
1.	My Lifelong Friend	1
2.	2oz of Sweets	5
3.	Drops	6
4.	Short Back and Sides	9
5.	Saturday Matinee	11
6.	Accident Prone	13
7.	Handful of Pennies	17
8.	My Rocking Horse	19
9.	Leftovers	23
10.	Jack Frost	25
11.	In all its Glory	28
12.	Suffering	30
13.	Laughter	31
14.	Maggoty Brook	33
15.	Family Puddings	35
16.	A Perfect Right Hand	38
17.	Dinners – One Day Only	40
18.	An Apple a Day	43
19.	My First Tram Ride	45
20.	Iron Horse	47
21.	Two Birthday Cards	49
22.	My First Car Ride	50
23.	Streamers	54

24.	Growing Another Head	56
25.	Iced Gems	58
26.	Peg Rugs	59
27.	Birmingham Post and Mail	60
28.	White Mice	63
29.	Share Number	65
30.	Saturday Pay Out	67
31.	Fares Please	69
32.	Playing Games with Brother John	71
33.	"Lonesome"	72
34.	Nailed	75
35.	Train Journey	76
36.	Our Duck Lonesome	80
37.	Cigarette Cards	82
38.	Being a Roundsboy	83
39.	Past Dreams	88
40.	The Rubbish Tip	90
41.	Tea Under the Apple Tree	93
42.	Tiddly Winks	96
43.	The Corn Shop	99
44.	Making Slides	101
45.	Land of the Spitfire	104
46.	Snow Hill Station	105
47.	In Awe	106
48.	Faithful Friends	107
49.	Butterflies	110
50.	Flying High	111
51.	Back Garden Adventure	114
52.	School Holidays	116
53.	The River Blythe	121
54.	Gas Works	124
55.	Trying to Make Both Ends Meet	129
56.	Ration Coupons	131

57.	Run Rabbit Run	134
58.	Jugs of Beer	140
59.	Pig Swill	141
60.	My Talking Boots	144
61.	Faggots and Peas	147
62.	All Grown Up	149
63.	Sixpence for Sweets	150
64.	Playing with Fire	152
65.	Dad's Works	154
66.	Fire Cans	156
67.	Heading House Bricks	158
68.	The Queen	160
69.	A Penny for Him	163
70.	Blood, Sweat and Tears	167
71.	Birmingham Hippodrome	172
72.	The Coal Merchants	173
73.	2/- to Spend	175
74.	Bags of Rags	177
75.	Playing Games	179
76.	One in the Eye	186
77.	Mine or Your Mom's	188
78.	Thursday Pictures	190
79.	Coach Trip	192
80.	Helping Brother	196
81.	The Boys' Brigade	199
82.	Scouts	200
83.	The Sea Cadets	202
84.	Two Black Poodles	203
85.	League Champions	207
86.	Bullying	210
87.	Down and Out	212
88.	Our Park	215
89.	Cycling	218

90. Paper Boy   221
91. Morning Dew   223
92. My Dad   227
93. Pawn Shop   229
94. Mom's Cake Stand   231
95. My Mom's Dear Friend Rita Hill   234
96. Shops Remembered   235
97. Disrespectful Children   237
98. Misdemeanours   239
99. A Big Thank You   241
100. To My Brothers and Sisters   242
101. A Poem by the Author   243
102. Becoming an Adult   244
103. Slang Phrases   245
     Appendix – by Trevor's son, Paul   247

ACKNOWLEDGEMENTS

My grateful thanks go to my ex-wife Irene, for patiently going through this book page by page correcting my spelling mistakes, of which there were many. When my memory needed a nudge, she was there to remind me, because I had told her so many times about my childhood. Irene has endured them from the tender age of sixteen, when we first met on 13th March 1960, she knows my childhood better than me. I owe it to her for encouraging me to sit down and write about my colourful life.

Putting together stories from my childhood brings back so many memories and images, not always good ones, but fondly remembered. The ones I have compiled in this book are the ones most vivid in my memory. There are, of course, many more but the ones I have written about I think are the most interesting.

* * *

My grateful thanks to the two artists for the line drawings they did throughout this book; Mr Alan Waite and Mr Graham Wilson.

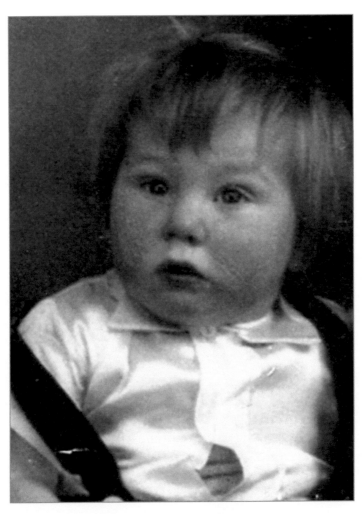

Me at the tender age of eighteen months.
Born on 30th October, 1943.

ABOUT THE AUTHOR

David is a real Brummie born to a very loving mother. His family lived in a council house in the Stechford area of Birmingham, where nearby there were fields, trees to climb, a river to play in and lots of places to explore.

He spent 1948 to 1958 at Audley Road School being very sporty, playing in goal at football and representing the school all through his school days, and he excelled at high jumping.

As a young boy, known as Pross to all his friends, he had a poor but very colourful childhood. His life was filled with many adventures that hopefully you will enjoy reading about.

Me with my sisters Kathleen, Janet and Doreen (left to right).

PHOTOS AND ILLUSTRATIONS

Me aged eighteen months   x
Me with my sisters   xii
Plowden Road and Swancote Road   xvi
My mom with her best friend Lizzie   2
Audley Road Secondary Modern School   2
The Infants' playground   3
The Senior School entrance   3
My first classroom on my first day at school   4
The wooden hut classrooms   4
The dreaded bridge to the Welfare Clinic   7
The Welfare Clinic   7
Illustration: *Not a leg to stand on*   16
Illustration: *Going too fast on my rocking horse*   21
My rocking horse   22
Illustration: *Apple scrumping for a pie*   37
Illustration: *An apple a day from teacher*   44
Illustration: *Scraping by*   51
The scene of my first car accident   52
Illustration: *Mrs Prosser, the chicken is pecking me*   74
Corona Bottles   86
Illustration: *Trying to become a road user*   91
Chelmsley Wood   94
Coronation Day, 2nd June 1953, my family   96
Street Party in Plowden Road   97
Illustration: *Biting the dust*   108
Illustration: *Balsa wood bi-plane attempt*   112
Illustration: *Beating Billy on my trolley*   119
Illustration: *A day at Coleshill*   122

Illustration: *Going to the Gas Works to get coke* 127
My shooting game Christmas present 136
Audley Road School – Infants' playground 137
The Juniors' playground and Headmaster's office 137
Showing the air raid shelters 138
Playground equipment 139
Illustration: *Watching the pigs* 143
Illustration: *Wishing for new boots* 146
Illustration: *Making our fire cans glow* 157
Illustration: *Author and Trevor waving to the Queen* 161
Bradford Hall and Chester Road (where we saw the Queen) 162
Illustration: *Some Guy in a pram* 165
The drive that Trevor and I dug out 170
Illustration: *Polly on the Mopstick* 179
Illustration: *British Bulldog* 181
Illustration: *Playing my favourite game – Football* 184
Illustration: *"Buy a raffle ticket, Lady?"* 205
Football League Champions 207
Illustration: *The only thing I was good at was high jumping* 208
Class of 1955 with teacher, Mr Lyceheart 209
Illustration: *Knocked out in the boxing ring* 214
Illustration: *My friends and I at Kenilworth Castle* 219
Illustration: *Enjoying the great outdoors* 225
My mom on a rare day out 232
Trevor and David – lifelong friends 248

YOUR LIFE

What makes life worthwhile?

As children we think that having lots of toys is the ultimate in life. But so is having lots of cuddles, being told you are nice, sitting with your family, walking together down a country lane and seeing Mother Nature. Looking at the trees, seeing the birds and knowing their names then learning to tell one from the other. To sit by a river and hear the sound of rippling water and feel the sun gently warming your back, to laugh and smile with your friends, to be with loved ones, to sit quietly sometimes and think how lucky you are.

The ultimate in life is to be told 'I love you' and for you to tell people you love them, these things in life cost nothing but fills the whole of your life with all the gifts you will ever need.

Plowden Road, my house is the last one on the right.

The bottom of Plowden Road,
where it meets Swancote Road, Trevor's road.

INTRODUCTION

I was born on 30th October 1943 at 38 Plowden Road, Glebe Farm, Birmingham 33. My mother was Dora Louisa Prosser (nee King), and Dad was William John Prosser, who everyone knew as Jack or Snowy because his hair went pure white at the age of 21.

We were a family of six at the time of my birth. My two eldest brothers went in the forces so I rarely saw them but I remember the times when I did see them, when they were on leave, for the pain I suffered at their hands. Then they got married. So, growing up until the age of five there were only four of us: me and my three sisters Kathleen, Doreen and Janet. My younger brother John was born five years after me.

My young life was surrounded by poverty and hardship, but after saying that, it bred into me a sense of make do and mend and survival. My mother was loving and caring she always put us first before herself but dad mostly thought of himself, the majority of his money went on drink and women, so he created the hardship we suffered.

Our house consisted of three bedrooms upstairs, downstairs was the living room, kitchen, pantry, bathroom, coal hole, a cubby hole under the stairs and a cupboard next to the bathroom. The Belfast sink in the kitchen was where Mom sat me as a child and bathed me more times than I remember. There was a wooden draining board that rested on the wall next to the sink and under the draining board was a boiler where Mom boiled up the water for us to have a bath if on that Saturday or Sunday evening she had three spare pennies for the gas meter. If not, we had no bath just a wash-down in the sink in the kitchen as at that time it was the only sink in the house. The water was lukewarm from the boiler behind the coal fire in the living room, if we had a fire that is, we weren't allowed to boil the kettle some of the time. As Mom could not let us use the gas when money was tight a wash down in cold water was okay in the summer but not so good in the winter. It was more difficult for the girls of course, us boys didn't like washing anyway, we tried to avoid washing no matter if the water was hot or cold. We had an outside toilet that wasn't so nice in the winter either.

I was a little terror, I often had cuts and broken bones, my mom had several names for me most of which I can't repeat. When I was born until the age of two, I was known as 'grizzle arse' because I cried and moaned so much my mom had to feed me continually, my wife says I haven't changed! Most children have one bottle at feed time but I always had two because my sister Janet, who is eighteen months older than me, was always hungry and my mom couldn't understand why this was, until one day she saw me taking Janet's bottle from her and drinking it all as well.

I was born two years before the end of the war so poverty for our family was there in all its glory and Dad, being unemployed since before the war, made all our lives even harder. It had taking my parents a long time to recover in the post war years so everything was 'make do and mend', meaning my life and my sisters' did not improve for many years. Mother, bless her, could do wonders with six pence (6d), buying spuds for 1d (one penny) a pound, veggies (2d) two pence a pound and 2d worth of bones from the butchers. I had to say they were for the dog, which we didn't have, but Mom fed us for days with all those vegetables in the form of what we called a stew.

I adored playing football, hopscotch, skipping, running, tip cat, table tennis, hot rice, kick the can, hide and seek, leap frog and any games going. At the age of four and a half I was playing in the horse road, drawing with a lump of chalk that was once a statue, with six girls Jacqueline Farrington, her sister Beryl, Rita Hill, Ann Hill, my two sisters Doreen and Janet, as there were no boys living by me at that time.

1. MY LIFELONG FRIEND

I was coming up to my fifth birthday and one afternoon I was sitting in the middle of the road opposite my front garden gate, drawing on the concrete road, I remember drawing a matchstick girl with a skirt on. My two sisters Doreen and Janet were playing with Ann Hill from across the road and the two girls from next door Beryl and Jacqueline, when I saw a lady walking down the road with a little boy. "Who is that lady?" I asked my sister Doreen. "They are moving into that empty house there," she said, pointing over the road. I was so excited at the thought of having a boy as a friend instead of soppy girls, well that's how I was thinking at that time in my life.

The next day I knocked on the door and asked if the little boy could come out and play. That day was the start of a lifelong friendship. We did a lot together from tatting (that's collecting metal) taking coach journeys, carrying coal, running errands, gardening and many, many more crazy things. We really enjoyed our childhood in spite of the poverty we grew up in. We were only interested in making money because we never got pocket money in those days.

His name was Trevor Kendall and we are friends to this very day. I can still remember that day I first saw him with his mother so well it's as clear to me like it was yesterday.

Trevor sadly passed away in 2021.

My mom (left) with her best friend Lizzie, Trevor's mom (right).

Audley Road Secondary Modern School. Showing the entrance from Swancote Road to the Infants' and Juniors' School Playgrounds. At the age of five, on my very first day of starting school, I walked up this entrance with my mom, across the Juniors' playground through the tunnel to the Infants' playground.

This was the Infants' playground. This tunnel is where my mom stood and watched me on my first day at school in 1948.

This was the entrance I had to use when I went into the Senior School, this entrance is off Audley Road.

This was my classroom on my first day at school.

This wooden hut was two classrooms. On the right was the Infants, on the left the Juniors. I was taught in both those classrooms, which have now been demolished. There were two doors in the middle with wooden steps leading up to them as you can see the doors and steps have been removed.

2. 2oz OF SWEETS

My earliest memory is when I was three years old, I used to stand on the windowsill to watch the children coming out of school, as we lived on the corner I had a clear view of the school entrance. I climbed on the chair, then the table to get to the windowsill. Mom always told me off for climbing but she never took me off the sill, I did it every day. The school entrance was half way up Swancote Road, just a bit further up the road were our local shops, which I went to every day with my mom because she had to buy cheap food for us all, I rarely got sweets.

One day I was playing my face, as my mom put it, for some sweets so she bought me 2oz of sweets, "Now don't tell your sisters you've had sweets." Being very greedy I ate them very quickly. My three sisters came home for their dinner at 1pm and as my sister Doreen walked in I immediately said, "I haven't had any sweets have I, Mom?" "Yes, you have or you wouldn't have said that," said Doreen, then she played her face something awful till Mom gave her a good hiding with a smacked bum. I was told I wouldn't be given any sweets again, nor was I.

It was a long time after that little episode, three years I bet, Mom bought some sweets and shared them between my two sisters Doreen and Janet and me. I thought I will wait for them to finish their sweets then I will start to eat mine it, was killing me not to eat mine. Then when they had finished theirs, I put a sweet in my mouth and made a sucking noise and said, "Mmm, these are nice." Doreen shouted, "Mom, he is playing us up with his sweets because we have eaten ours!" "I know, I heard him," said Mom, so with a smack across the back of my head, my sweets were taken off me and shared between my two sisters, I ended up with nothing. Well only the one I had in my mouth that I had been tormenting my sisters with. I cried my little heart out, but I never did it again, once bitten as the saying goes.

3. DROPS

I was about three years old when once a week my mom would take me to a welfare clinic which was situated in Kitts Green. I remember the first time I went to that clinic I had drops down my ears, throat, up my nose and in my eyes. I've no idea what was wrong with me and I never thought to ask my mom as the years passed, I think I just wanted to forget about it. So, whenever I was taken to the clinic I screamed and fought like my life depended on it, the nurse would say, "If you're good you can have a bottle of this orange juice," smacking her lips to show me how nice it was. That bribe worked every time, I always was thick! Unbeknown to me she would give my mom a bottle of cod liver oil which she hid away from me. I was held down at home to be given a spoonful of that horrid cod liver oil (they would have to hold me down these days as well!). After, I was always given a spoonful of orange juice straight away, I loved that welfare orange juice it was thick and sweet.

Mom's friend Winnie called at our house one morning with her son John who also became my friend. Mom said, "Come on son, we're going for a walk." That excited me and as we were walking, I kept asking, "Where are we going?" She said, "Just for a walk, son." As we turned the corner I saw the bridge, I then knew what was on the other side of that bridge, the welfare clinic where hurt and pain lay. I pulled, shouted and cried very loudly, if I could have got free of Mom's grip I would have run off. I was what these days is known as 'throwing a wobbly', "Please, Mommy," I was saying, "Don't take me in there." Every time I saw that bridge, I threw a wobbly, even to this very day when I see that bridge I get a horrible feeling in the pit of my stomach, those feelings do not seem to want to leave me.

Mothers in those days used to get baby food called National Dried Milk, free for their children. I don't think there was an air raid shelter,

The dreaded bridge to the Welfare Clinic.

The Welfare Clinic.

shed, coalhouse or pantry that hadn't got a National Dried Milk tin in there, I've seen them with nails, screws, tools, drills, car bits, motorbike bits, you name it those tins housed it. We had a couple of those tins in our house I was informed by my better half. National Dried Milk full cream was a silver tin then later white with blue writing. Half cream was silver and again later white with red writing. I have even seen those tins made into toys, I've seen a lorry and a train, I bet there are hundreds still out there in the shape of every toy you can think of, I want one!

4. SHORT BACK AND SIDES

The first time I went to the barbers I was only four and a half years old and Mom took me for a haircut known as a short back and sides. The name of the barbers was Tranters, as Mom walked in with me and explained what she wanted him to do, Mr Tranter said, "Leave him here while you do your shopping."

I said, "I don't want my hair cut, mom."

"You'll be okay son," she said and off she went shopping. I was terrified.

Well, Mr Tranter fought with me to get me into that chair. Just when he thought he had won, he was puffing and blowing, I jumped out of that chair and ran into the street outside to find my mom. He came running after me and caught hold of my arm, so I kicked him as hard as I could. I cannot print what he said to me! He dragged me back inside, threw me into the chair and I mean threw, I must have bounced about two feet into the air. With a very loud voice he yelled down my ear, "Now sit still!" So I did because he scared me. Comb and scissors no problem. I remember thinking this is all right then he turned the electric clippers on and started to shave by my ear. I flew out of that chair, ducked under his arms and ran outside with the sheet still wrapped around me. He got hold of me so I kicked him again, he shook me and dragged me back into the shop. He was much rougher with me that time than the time before, again I was thrown back into that chair, I think I bounced four feet that second time. He said to me, "Okay son, I won't use the electric clippers I will only use the comb and scissors." I was still terrified but I calmed down when the scissors were being used.

So, finally, I got my haircut. When he had finished cutting, he put me on a chair where all the men were sitting waiting for their hair to be cut. The room was full of cigarette smoke, it was like sitting in a fog, my eyes were smarting and it made me cough. They were talking about football. I remember there were three men cutting hair, those same men were there for years. It was a dark mysterious sort of room, well to a youngster anyway, dark oak panels everywhere. The ladies were on the left as you walked in, a narrow passage led to the men's at the back room. Mom walked in looked at me and said, "That's a nice hair cut son, you do look smart. Has he been okay, Mr Tranter?"

"Yes, Mrs Prosser he was fine." She paid him, I think it was 6d (six pence).

"Bye, David," he said as he patted me on the back of my head very hard. "Come again," he said, as we walked out the other barbers started laughing, they knew he didn't really want to see me again. My mom never knew till years later what that poor barber went through.

5. SATURDAY MATINEE

The first Saturday matinee I ever went to was at the Atlas Cinema in Stechford, Birmingham, about 400 yards or so just down the road from my house. I went with my sister Doreen and my mom gave her strict instructions not to take me to the back of the cinema where the tip was and not to go through the park after the films had finished.

It was like a stampede to get out, I had never seen so many screaming kids. Doreen took me over the tip, the one Mom said not to, as I got much older I spent many hours on that tip, my sister said, "Don't tell Mom we came the park way home."

As we walked over the tip, we came across a big hole at the edge with a corrugated sheet of metal across one corner of it, someone had been making a den. "I'm going inside," Doreen said, "you stand there and don't stand on this tin it's not safe." As she went in, I looked at the tin sheet and thought it's okay, I won't fall if I stand on it, so I stood on it. It swivelled because it was resting on two opposite corners and I fell into the hole catching my inside left knee on the corner of the tin sheet, it sliced though my leg like butter, the blood was cascading down my leg, the cut was an inch wide and about three inches long.

Thinking a lump of flesh had come out, me and Doreen were searching for it so we could put it back in the hole and it would heal up and be okay. "It's gone Dave," she said, "come on, I'll take you to the park keeper." She wrapped her handkerchief round my leg, with the blood still cascading down. When the Parkie (that's what everyone called him) saw my leg he went white. He wrapped it up with loads of bandages, but the blood came through as soon as he put it on, "You must take him straight to the hospital, that's a very bad cut," he said. In those days the park keepers only had push bikes so he couldn't take me to the hospital.

Doreen was crying by this time and I was very pale, losing my strength to walk and feeling very poorly. Doreen had to carry me home so she too got covered in blood. Poor Mom had a shock when she saw me and Doreen covered in blood, "Oh my god! My baby what have you done now?" I can remember my mom saying that, why I have no idea. I can't remember any more, whether it's because I passed out from loss of blood, I'm not sure. I had eleven stitches and the scar is still very visible even now. I've never known to this day if Doreen got a good hiding or not, I have discussed it with her since and I asked her if she can remember getting a belting off Mom but she can't remember. I'm sure if Mom had belted her, she would have remembered.

6. ACCIDENT PRONE

Every summer holiday when I was off school for six weeks my mom, bless her, would pray and ask the Lord, "Please lord don't let David hurt himself this holiday." I was accident prone. It started when I was four years old just before I started school. In our back garden we had a lean to shed with a flat roof, constructed by my older brother Donald. The shed had a chicken pen incorporated in it and, as children do, we climbed on the shed and jumped off it for what we thought was fun and enjoyment. There was me, my two sisters Doreen and Janet and their friend Rita Hill, it was 1947 and it had been raining so the ground was very muddy. I was too scared to jump so my sister Janet (she told me many years later) pushed me.

When I hit the ground I did the splits and I heard a crack, the pain was so bad that I lay in the mud screaming. My mom was up the road shopping so my sister Kathleen carried me into the house. A neighbour came in to see if she could help, "Where does it hurt?" she asked me. I'm lying on the settee in agony and she asked where does it hurt, by this time the house was full of people, another lady kept touching my leg asking, "Does it hurt there?"

I said, "Yes, yes!" every time she touched me. I heard her say to a woman next to her, "He is stupid, he is saying it hurts no matter where I touch him." It did.

My mom came rushing in, "Oh my baby! What have you done, son?" she was hurting more than I was, "I must take him to the hospital." Mom had no money for the bus fare, she tried to borrow the money but no one had any. The people where we lived, well all the ones I ever knew, were not much better off than my family. My cousin Arthur was living with us at that time (because his mom whose name was Margaret and was my mom's sister was killed in the bombing in the Second World

War, she lived at number 53 Ash Road, Saltley) and when he came home from work he said, "I'll take him on the bus to the hospital and give my name and address." That was the done thing then when people had no money. "Okay, you do that. Take him to the accident hospital and I'll meet you there as soon as I can," said Mom.

I found that if I kept my leg bent in a permanent position it was less painful, so my cousin took me on the number 14 bus to town. We got off the bus in the old square (Birmingham city centre), we waited a while, then Arthur and I got back on the bus. Why we did that I have no idea and neither did Arthur, we got back off the bus at Alum Rock and sat on the wall outside a factory called Southhalls. Why he did what he did I have never known, neither did my mom, he could have taken me to any hospital. As we sat on the wall, my mom passed on the bus, she spotted Arthur sitting on the wall. Full of panic and anger she got off at the next stop, ran down the road to where she had seen Arthur. My cousin had not seen Mom as the bus passed so he crossed us over the road and we got back on the next bus and he took me back home.

When Mom got to Southhalls only to find he had gone she asked a lady if she had seen a man carrying a little boy? "Yes," she said pointing, "he has just got on that bus that is disappearing round the bend." Mom, too, headed back home crying. As she walked into the living room and flopped into the chair saying to Arthur, "Why did you bring him back home?" My cousin replied, "I didn't know what to do." He wasn't very bright. Mom was worn out, she took a deep breath and said, "I can't do any more today, I will take him myself tomorrow."

So I was in agony all night, Mom said I couldn't have any aspros as I was too young. Still with my leg bent, next day at the hospital the doctor asked, "When did he break his leg?"

"This morning, Doctor," she replied.

"I don't think so, it's started to set. I think he did this last night. Wait outside, mother," he told her. "I will look after him," he said with a smile as he led Mom out of the room. He put his right hand at the back of my left foot, his left hand on the front of my knee, pushed down with his left hand and up with his right, did I scream! Mom came running in, "My baby! My baby! What are you doing to him?"

"It's all right mother, I've only straightened his leg," he said as though it was nothing. "Now we can X-ray it, he is a big strong boy, mother." That didn't help the pain.

It turned out I had dislocated my ankle and my knee cap and cracked the long bone up the front of my leg from the foot to the knee. I have no recollection of getting an injection, I would remember if I had as I hate injections. My leg was plastered and I was asked if I wanted a walking stick or a pair of crutches, so I asked for a pair of crutches. The nurse said, "Come with me David, I will show you how to use the crutches," so in the corridor she showed me the best way to use them. Feeling very weak and tired out, I found it very difficult to lift my plastered leg and the nurse started to lose her patience with me. "Lift your leg you are leaving chalk marks all along the corridor," she said in, well how can I put it, an excitable sort of voice. When I looked around it looked like those broken white lines you see in the middle of the road. When Mom came to collect me the nurse's voice went very calm, "Bye David," she said, "you are a brave little boy. He will be all right, mother," she said as she put her hand on Mom's shoulder. That two-faced nurse. My mom would have been very angry if she had heard her speaking to me in the manner in which she did.

We went back into the waiting room and waited what seemed like forever when a man called out "Ambulance for Mrs Prosser." We got into the ambulance and you know I can remember that ambulance ride like it was only last week, I loved it. All the children that came to see me had a play with my crutches, they had so much fun with them as they did when playing games in the street. I wish I could say my mom was happy but maybe I really wish I hadn't given my mom so many problems.

At the age of four if you don't do as you are told by your mother, this is what can happen to you. I never did as I was told and look what happened to me!

7. HANDFUL OF PENNIES

I loved going to the fair, it was always and still is in the same place, we always called it the Bull's Head Fair in Stechford. The Bull's Head was a public house one hundred yards from the fair, I say was because it has now been demolished like so many other public houses in the area.

I'd only had my broken leg out of plaster for a week and I was going to the fair with Trevor and Tony (Trevor's brother). We got off at the bus stop after the Atlas Cinema, it was evening time and the road was very busy, I suppose they were coming out of work. Tony and Trevor ran across the road, I looked across and Tony shouted "Stay there!" but I thought the road was clear. I ran across the road gripping my 11d (eleven pennies) in my hand, a car hit me and I went up in the air doing a somersault. I landed on my back, my head bounced off the concrete road and the car had hit my left leg (the one I'd had in plaster) how it never broke again I will never know. The man driving the car was shaking, "Get in the car," he said to me, he didn't know what he was saying, and then he said, "Get out of the car," so out I got. I was very shaken, but fortunately not hurt, even though I was crying my little heart out by this time and I had a big lump on the back of my head.

A lady came up to me and said, "Here you are son, I've picked your pennies up for you, here is your nine pence." "There was eleven pennies," I said. "That's all I found," she answered. I'm not making up excuses because I had been in a road accident but my manners were bad, I never even said thank you to that kind lady for picking up my pennies, all I could think about was getting to the fair. The traffic by this time was well backed up and there were crowds watching me, I was famous for ten minutes.

I limped off to the fair to spend my 9d and the man drove off, I bet it took him a long time to get over that accident, poor man. After a few minutes at the fairground, I soon forgot all about it. I'm lucky to be alive. You know I never ever as the years passed told my mom about that accident, I thought she had been through enough with me as a child. Plus, if I had told her she would have never let me go to the fair again. I think I must have been a tough little fellow.

8. MY ROCKING HORSE

On my fourth birthday I was given a rocking horse, I remember being so excited, I also remember my sisters were playing on it and wouldn't get off and let me get on it. I stood there crying my little heart out. Mom came into the living room from the kitchen and told them to get off it, boy I was very happy. My sister Janet would be on the back, Doreen on the front with me in the middle, we had a great time. I will never know how that rocking horse stood up to the treatment we gave it, we treated it very roughly but it was a toy after all and I enjoyed playing on it for many years. I was Hopalong Cassidy one day, Roy Rogers the next, Tex Ritter another, my imagination ran wild. There was one drawback to that rocking horse if I tried rocking too fast the back legs came up, locked and threw me over its head.

My mom kept that horse in the coal house which had a brick-built shelf with concrete slabs on the top which was covering the water pipes, my rocking horse went on there. It just fitted but the trouble was it got black from the coal dust, when we had coal that is. If I came off that horse because I rocked too fast Mom would say, "I told you didn't I if you came off it, I would put it back in the coal house, you little bugger," she always called me that, "you will break your bloody neck one of these days," she would say. Every few days I would ask if I could have my horse out to play with, a lot of times she said, "no" because it needed cleaning and she was busy getting the dinners ready for my sisters to have when they came out of school at dinner time.

When I did get to play on it, Mom would once again say, "if you come off it, back in the coalhole, now be warned young man." I came off it and back it went. I usually got a nice big lump on my forehead from hitting the floor or the wall. Okay, I would think after Mom had put it back in the coalhole, I will ride my pretend horse and much to the annoyance of my mother I would hold out my left arm as though I was holding the horse's reins and slapping my backside with my right hand, I would gallop around the house. I was the sheriff, a cowboy, an Indian and outlaw all rolled into one. I think Mom sometimes wished she had let me play in the living room with my rocking horse.

My dad had made the horse. He got all the wood from his works at the Metropolitan Camel Carriage Works in Saltley, where he was a Radial Driller. How Dad got the wood out I have no idea, it was all cut to shape when he brought it out. It was well-seasoned timber, the same as they used when building the railway carriages, that's what Dad's firm made everything to do with railways. My mom's brother Bob, my uncle of course, was a manager at the same works; whether he helped my dad get the wood I've no idea or he could have bought it as scrap from the firm. I know you could buy scrap from them in those days.

The metal rockers, or 'stays' as my dad called them, were made from 5/16 of an inch round steel which were also bent to shape. Dad did tell me he had a few goes at making the rocking horse before he got it right. He made mine for my birthday and then four other horses for our neighbours' children for Christmas, as my birthday was in October and the neighbours had seen my horse they asked him to make one for each of their children, how much he charged I have no idea. He had time to make all the horses for Christmas. He got everything he needed from work to complete all the horses even the paint, but he ran out of paint for the last horse so he borrowed the paint from work. He used to put it in jam jars as they fitted in the old army bag he used to take his sandwiches in, he would put the strap over his head so it hung down his left side. He made the mistake of getting paint that needed a coat of special varnish to make it dry, but he didn't know this at the time and after Christmas one of the fathers complained, saying his daughter on Christmas morning got paint all over her and ruined her new clothes. My horse was okay, he must have used the right paint for mine.

Janet, my sister, had my rocking horse for twenty years. My brother John made a pattern of it and made some horses, he gave me one so I

*Every time I played on my rocking horse, I would go too fast and was
thrown over its head. I always got told off by my mom
and the horse was put back in the coal house.*

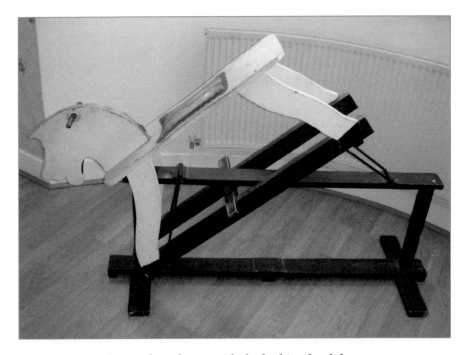

My rocking horse with the locking back legs.

took it to Janet's and swapped it for my horse which now sits in the corner of my bedroom, every time I look at it the memories of my childhood are fondly remembered. You can see from the pictures how the legs locked and threw me over its head. The reason I let Janet have the horse for so long was I was living in rooms at that time and I couldn't take it with me. My kids never played on it and when I think about it now that makes me sad.

9. LEFTOVERS

I have heard people say that when they were children the food their parents ate always seemed better than what they were given. I was just the same. My dad would come home from work, which was usually late because he always dropped into the Tote, which was a club by his works. Dropped in means he was drinking before he came home. When he sat down to dinner I used to stand and watch him eating, this used to annoy him. "What do you want?" he would say in a stern voice. "Can I have some meat please?" I would ask and he would hand me his fork with a lump of meat on it, and with an angry look say "Gad Blimey." That was his favourite saying and the other two words that went with that I just cannot repeat, or do not wish to in print, it was his way of saying, I am annoyed. He would put a piece of spud on the end of his fork as he handed it to me, it always tasted much better to me than mine just because it was Dad's.

I would stand there chewing and he then would order me to go and play, so I always went into the kitchen waited a couple of minutes and strolled back into the living room and sat on the settee, this was facing forward to where the dining table was. I just kept a low profile, thinking he wouldn't notice. When he had finished eating, he would always push his plate away from him and wipe his fingers on the tablecloth. Quick as a flash I would jump up and look on Dad's plate to see if anything was left if there was, I would say, "Please can I have that, Dad?" I had to be quick for fear someone else in the room would get there before me, "Go on," he would say as he rose from the dining room chair to the easy chair by the fire. No matter what was left I ate it, greedy no, hungry yes I was.

As soon as Dad sat in his easy chair by the fire, he lit up his Woodbine cigarette. As it got dark the flickering flames from the fire danced all over the ceiling, an image that holds such special memories for me, feeling very secure and cosy. I would play 'I Spy' with my sisters, we only had a wireless (we didn't have a television for several years). Playing 'I Spy' was a laugh because I couldn't read and my sisters would say, "I spy with my little eye something beginning with H." I would say, "Door, window, rug…" They were very patient with me.

I also remember a lot of times when the fire was just a glow in the grate and kept alive by putting one lump of coal on at a time, it was those times when I went out and pulled the palings off the neighbours' fences for firewood. When we did have five hundred weight of coal delivered, on a Sunday Mom would "have a nice fire going." When evening came the curtains were drawn and once again those flickering dancing images on the ceiling, even on the walls, on a cold winter's night would warm me right through.

Many times, we would all sit in the dark with just the fire aglow, Kathleen, Doreen, Janet, John in his pram, Mom, Dad and me. Dad smoking his Woodbine, my mom would be knitting most evenings when all was quiet, the clicking of the knitting needles sounded very loud, the rest of us just staring into the fire not a word being said. It's a warm feeling remembering those family evenings. When I'm sitting in my lounge with the light off and the glow from my open fire is dancing on the ceiling it takes me back to those wonderful days sitting with my mom, dad, brother and sisters, it's a warm feeling I'm getting typing up this page. Go on close your eyes and think back to your childhood and remember the happy times in your life with your family then you will be at ease with life. The best time, I find, is when one is alone and quiet, even fond memories of friends playing in the street will bring fond memories flooding into one's memory.

10. JACK FROST

Every year when winter came around our house was very cold and damp. Every morning as we were returning to the land of the living we knew it was very cold outside because our breath would look like steam coming out of the boiling kettle. Even the cup sitting on the floor which had water in it would be frozen ice, the bed clothes were wrapped even tighter around us to keep in the warmth. Our mother had one hell of a job getting us out of bed. One thing I do remember well, were the beautiful patterns in the ice on the inside of our windows, the colours were sparkling when the early morning sun shone on them, the ice was so thick when I tried to scratch it with my nail nothing happened. I couldn't make a hole in the ice to see what the weather was like outside.

I always hoped it had snowed. I loved playing in the snow even though I was never properly clad for such an event. We had lino on the floor and when I got out of bed half asleep and put my foot on the floor, I soon woke up it was like standing on ice. I only possessed one shirt, I hadn't any pyjamas, so I slept in my shirt sometimes even my socks were left on. I slept with my younger brother and he wet the bed every night, so every morning I was soaking wet. My mom lit the oven so we could stand in front of it to get dry, the steam rising off my shirt smelled of drying urine, very unpleasant.

I had to go to school every day with that same shirt on. I tucked my collar inside my shirt so I could wash my neck. One shirt, a pair of pumps with holes in, my socks had more holes in them than there was material, a coat I could not fasten because it was too small, that was my entire wardrobe. We only possessed one towel in our house at that time in my life and for a long time after that, being the two youngest when we came to use the towel it was soaking wet. On a very cold snowy or frosty winter's morning feeling very cold and drying oneself on a wet towel was to say the least, not nice. Mom would say "You will be all right, dry yourself." I went through that type of life longer than I care to remember. It must have been heart breaking for my mom. We had a long blue family comb, which sat on the windowsill next to the back door; again, we only had one and it was used by the whole family. We had that comb for years, it was made of nylon, before that the combs we had were plastic and the teeth broke off within a week.

I got two slices of toast most mornings and on rare occasions we got porridge. All through my school years I took two pieces of toast for my lunch wrapped in some of the bread paper, I put them in my coat pocket and by break time they were all screwed up like someone had twisted them round. Funny really thinking about it, I always really enjoyed that toast I can smell it and taste it as I'm typing up this page, I bet as you are reading this chapter you wished you had lived like I did!

Years earlier I slept in a bed with my two sisters, they were at the top of the bed and I was at the bottom. Yes, we had arguments about feet every night, most times I put my cold feet on them, I did it on purpose I loved playing them up. In the winter sometimes Mom put a house brick in the oven, wrapped it up in a pillow case, and put it in the bed so that it felt very cosy, even a pop bottle filled with warm water was used when we had one. On occasions the water would leak out of the bottle and wet the bed because we hadn't screwed the stopper up tight enough.

It was rare for us to have pop and if we did when the bottle was empty it was taken back because there was a deposit on the pop bottle. I've taken them back to get the deposit for my mom then bought two pounds of spuds with the 2d at first, then it went up to 3d (three pence) which I got off the bottle.

When my eldest brother came home on leave from the army his overcoat was put on our bed, it felt very heavy and very warm. I was told many times by my mom, "There are people out there worse off than you, are," all I can say to that is they must have been naked and lived in a cave.

Our toilet, being outside, froze up every winter. My mom took a bucket to bed with her and we all would go into her bedroom to use it because we wouldn't go outside in the freezing cold. Crossing the landing we shivered all the way there and back. My mom worked so hard for her children, as most mothers do, she was always first up and suffered those cold Jack Frost bitten mornings to warm the kitchen up for all her family do the breakfast for us and Dad's lunch for work. As we all left school and joined the ranks of workers, Mom still did the same every morning but then she had lunches to do as well. How those mothers cope, I have no idea, but my hat goes off to those brave ladies all of them.

11. IN ALL ITS GLORY

Next door to our house lived Barry and his parents, sometimes they took me with them when they had a picnic and the males, including Barry, would go fishing. On one trip I fell in the river at Coleshill and Barry's dad took us home in his Scammel Scarab, his three-wheeled LMS Railway Iron Horse, but more about that later!

On another picnic with Barry and his family we all got on the number 14 bus at Glebe Farm, where we went to I've no idea, but we were there all day fishing. I wandered off because I didn't like fishing, still don't, I get bored. There was a barbed wire fence surrounding what I thought was a wood. What's in there, I thought, so under the wire I went catching my trousers on the barbed wire I heard the sound of ripping material. Well, it had torn my trousers how can I say, like an upside-down U, it made a flap. I had no underpants on (the reason being that I didn't possess any) so I tucked in the hanging piece of material the best I could, to make sure no one could see my bare rear. I headed back to where they were fishing and sat on the grass next to them, making sure my flap was tucked in and hoping they wouldn't see it.

When all was packed up, off we went heading for home, me walking at the side of them holding my trousers where they were ripped. On the bus ride home I was enjoying all that a boy likes to see, toy shops and my mind was full of all sorts as I gazed out of the window, which made me forget all about my ripped trousers. I got off the bus, not a thought about my trousers, and I was walking in front of Barry's parents and they were all laughing. I looked round to see why they were laughing, Barry's mom holding her stomach while in fits of laughter said in a muffled voice through the laughter, "What have you done to your trousers, David?" By this time, they were all in fits of laughter, Barry's two sisters, his older brother Ronny and his mom and dad but Barry wasn't laughing he was more concerned for me. Of course, I was showing both cheeks of my bare bum, I must have looked a sight, my face felt hot and I went red. On arriving home my mom was not too pleased as she had to find something to patch those trousers for me to wear when I went back to school. The only material she had was red so the patch was red on my grey trousers, she had tried very hard to find some material that was suitable, and Mom even asked her friend Lizzie (Trevor's mom) but she didn't have anything suitable, so mom had to use the red patch as they were the only ones I possessed.

Even though we lived in poverty I had a wonderful childhood, my mother always did the best she could for her family. It's easy to criticise when one is brought with better living standards. I always remember my mom saying if you only have a penny you cannot spend two.

12. SUFFERING

I remember one very cold winter's evening in 1949 or 1950 and the fire in the grate was only just glowing, the five of us were very cold. Mom was rubbing our hands and giving us a cuddle to warm us up, Dad was nowhere to be seen. Mom was crying because her little children were cold and hungry, it was very hard for a child to see. I wanted to help, I remember thinking I wish I could help my mom, so I sat and thought of ways I could help, then it came to me.

That evening started me on to pulling off the palings in my garden as well as up and down my road. It was snowing and without gloves my hands soon got cold, I had no overcoat, no wellingtons, and only worn-out pumps. The fences in our area were low, it was feather-edge fencing about two and a half feet high, all the front gardens at that time had the same fencing it was put there by the council. I was able to pull off the palings which were about four inches wide, the nails were rotting and some came away with no trouble, others I had to use one of the palings as a lever to prise them off. With an armful I took them home thinking Mom would be pleased, but I got a severe telling off and told, "Never take what isn't yours." I cried like a baby, she kissed and hugged me. After that I used to break them up and put them in the coalhouse when we had no coal, so I knew Mom wouldn't go in there. I became quite good at getting those palings off. At the end of that winter the palings in my road had a lot of gaps.

Mom asked me to go to the tip to find some old shoes so she could burn them on the fire, 'shoes to burn' well I thought Mom had lost the plot. With slack and potato peelings they made a good fire. I found many shoes on the tip, I even went there with my friend Trevor we had a sack each, our new goal in life was to find old shoes for our mothers to burn. I made a trolley and a bike off that tip but that's another story. I can say though, I loved my childhood, the freedom to roam and to explore, I am very grateful for that.

13. LAUGHTER

When my mom used to tell me my eldest brother Donald was coming home on leave from the army, I used to shake with fear. I think he loved to hear screams with pain attached to them, but only if they were from other people, I think if it had been him in pain, he would not have done it to others. Mom would say, "Oh that's good," as she read his letter, "he's coming home for the weekend." "Oh no," I used to think to myself. I used to try and hide and stay out of his way.

When I was out playing, I completely forgot about Donald coming home from the army. In I went to have my tea through the back kitchen and into the living room. Then absolute total fear stormed through my little body, as sitting on the chair behind the living room door was Donald. "Got you!" he would say as he grabbed my arm. "You forgot about me didn't you," he would say. "Have you been playing up?" he would ask. "No," I would reply. He would turn me over his knee and bite my bum. I'm not going to cry, I used to think to myself, but the pain was unbearable. I held back the tears then he would say, "Oh tough are we now!" Over his knee again and boy did he bite. "YES!" I screamed very loud and cried for a long time. I had big teeth marks and very bad bruising, it was tender and very sore for a long time, even sitting was a problem for me. He laughed very loud and thought it was funny, I didn't think it was funny.

It turned out he had been told not to hit the kids by my mom (Donald told me that years later when I questioned him about the bullying). He would say "Well I haven't hit him, I only bit his bum." One afternoon my two eldest brothers were throwing my sister Janet up to the ceiling and catching her as she was coming down, she was laughing and having a good time, enjoying every moment of it. I would say, "My turn, do it to me, do it to me," so they threw me up in the air, I hit the ceiling and they turned and walked away. I hit the floor and started to cry from the pain but they seemed to think this was very funny as the two of them were laughing. Mom said, "Why don't you leave him alone." Donald replied, "We're only playing, he's alright." It seemed they thought what they did to me didn't matter.

14. MAGGOTY BROOK

I was aged five when my sister Doreen, aged eight maybe nine, took me and my sister Janet aged six over the park to what was called the white bridge, so called because it was painted white. This was in the Bucklands End area, the road name was Colehall Lane. At that time in 1948 all the new houses were being built and we explored the unfinished houses as they didn't have doors fitted so it wasn't a problem getting in. It was fun to me, I had never seen houses being built and I was really fascinated. Just by the end house was the River Cole, the white bridge spanned it of course, and about eight yards from the bridge was a fresh water spring, known as Maggoty Brook. Everyone, well all the children, called it that but I've no idea why or who gave it that name. We all drank from that flowing clear spring water, I myself on many occasions drank from it as I was growing up.

All those houses I saw being built at the age of five have in the last couple of years been demolished and now new houses stand where they were, that's such a short time for houses to be knocked down 1948 to 2008. I wonder if Maggoty Brook is still there? I must go and look and relive my memory as a five-year-old. By the way, the white bridge is no longer there. One year we had very bad storms and the swollen river broke its banks, lifted that old white bridge, and turned it sideways which made it float down the river. A temporary bridge was erected, single line traffic only, traffic lights each end of it. I was told it was temporary, but it is still there years later. I wonder how much longer it will be there across the river, will it outlive the new houses? At least it slows the traffic down which is a good thing, especially at night as it is very dark in that area. After writing this chapter that bridge has been taken down and a beautiful bridge now stands there, it's a credit to whoever constructed it.

My sister had a den under all the overhanging trees, brambles and shrubs on the river's edge. It was great, I really loved it. I went there a few times with a friend of mine to think when I was six years old, being allowed to go all over the place. I would play in the river and to think it was full of pollution, they used to allow the sewage into that river instead of into the sewage farm which was next to it. All Mom used to say and she said it all the time was, "Mind the horse road" and "Behave yourself" and those sayings never changed. I bet those sayings are still said today by some of the older generation to young children. Mom would say things like, "Where have you been?" The answer was always, "Nowhere." Mom would usually ask, "What you been doing?" Our reply was always, "Nothing." "I don't know, you have been out all day, been nowhere and done nothing," she always replied. Been down the park to me was going nowhere, playing, was doing nothing, not like running errands or going up to town.

So many things we did as children that as adults give us such wonderful memories to look back on, especially in the evening sitting alone in a darkened room with just the reflection of the coal fire flickering and dancing round the room, like the evenings when we sat with our mother. What wonderful feelings run through my body when remembering those halcyon days. What freedom, boy was I a lucky little lad. Of course, as a child I didn't realise how lucky I was to have such freedom.

15. FAMILY PUDDINGS

Mom was a wonderful cook, self-taught on most recipes, but my nan of course showed her how to do many dishes. Her bread pudding was so tasty, I used to help her to mix it up because I loved the feel of that mixture on my hands. We sometimes had fruitcake but I was never allowed to mix or touch that mixture. My brothers and sisters used to stand around the kitchen table watching Mom mix and stir the mixture, we all waited for the remnants left in the bowl. We would fight to see who could get the bowl and scrape out the mixture that was left. If I was lucky enough to be there on my own, Mom used to let me scrape out the bowl all by myself.

The food I didn't like eating was tripe, chitterlings, brains, kidneys and liver. Even if I was hungry, I wouldn't eat those items of food. Apple pies were my favourite, it was fascinating to watch Mom doing the pastry. She used to use a sterilised milk bottle as a rolling pin, sprinkling flour everywhere, it used to be all over the floor and all over Mom's pinny, I can see her doing that now. I would help to peel the apples, I used to eat all the apple peel, the core, pips as well even the stalk if it was still there in the apple. All the pastry that was left after doing the apple pie, Mom used to allow one of us to make jam cakes with it. She always put a pattern around the pies and a pattern in the middle, also a slit in the middle to let the steam out. I used to feel very clever when I made the jam cakes with the leftover pastry and say to my sisters, "I've made this." My mom used to make me share them. When she made mince pies after rolling out the pastry, she would get a set of metal cutters that she bought from Woolworths for 6d (sixpence). She always allowed her children to use the cutters to cut the shapes out of the pastry it was very exciting for me to see the shapes they made.

Another pudding I used to love was suet pudding, known as Spotted Dick. After mixing the pudding Mom would place it into a pillow case or a tea towel and put it into a pan of water to boil. One pudding I hated was Yorkshire pudding with jam on it. I used to eat it but never liked it. I was never keen on rice pudding either but I loved semolina and still do.

Another food item that I did like that Mom made was brawn. Mom used to buy pigs' heads from the butcher's, scrub them clean, put her fingers in the eyeball sockets and pull out the eyes. The head was then boiled in a pan and that was one smell I hated. The brawn, when it was done and set, was even better than when it was brought from the butchers. Cooking is one thing that I have never taken to, I used to watch my mom do all the baking and all the ingredients were never measured, she just guessed them. She was so good she got the weight close enough to the nearest ounce.

If we knew Mom was going to bake the next day, my sister Janet and Trevor's sister Nanette, Trevor and myself would go scrumping apples when it was dark.

The one time I remember, as we crept out of one of the back gardens, my sister Janet had filled her knickers with apples, me and Trevor put them down our shirts and Nanette, to our amazement, was dragging behind her a branch full of apples. When we asked her why she had broken off a branch she replied, "I couldn't be bothered picking the apples and filling my knickers with them so I broke off this branch." We were all surprised at the number of apples that were on the branch, we ate some of the apples and we took the rest to our moms. Our moms always told us off but seeing that we couldn't take them back Mom made a beautiful apple pie. Of course, it always depended on whether Mom had enough flour, lard, eggs and whatever else one needs to make pies with, usually we got our pie.

"Okay Trev that's enough, I hope they are sweet.
I'll take some home to my mom – she might make an apple pie."
"Yeah, me too, Dave. I'll take some to my mom as well."

16. A PERFECT RIGHT HAND

In 1949 I had been in school for about seven months, I started in the January of that year, a tender five-year-old. I was asked with all the other boys and girls to take home a letter telling my parents about a day out at Whipsnade Zoo, and would they sign the consent form to allow their sons or daughters to go on the coach and would they pay 3d (three pence) a week or more as the cost of the trip was 10/- (ten shillings). I don't recall paying the 3d every week, I do however, remember saying to my teacher on one occasion that I hadn't any money to give to her and she shouted at me in a very loud voice and shamed me in front of the whole class, by saying that all the other boys and girls had paid, so why couldn't I? What did they expect a five-year-old to do at that time when children relied on their parents, it was all my mom could do to feed us.

Anyway, I did go on the trip, my teacher and the headmistress came with us. I can still see that screwed-up face of that headmistress, I hated her, talk about ruling a child with a rod of iron. That headmistress had two iron rods and a whip, her voice was the whip and her hands were the rods of iron, her right-hand slap could make you have nightmares for a fortnight. I remember nothing of the day at Whipsnade Zoo, only one incident that is burned in my memory, I can't remember that headmistress's name nor do I want to.

There was a fairground ride which had a barrier all round it so no one could walk into the ride and get hurt. Being five years old and very small I put my hands on top of the rail and ducked my head under it. I was about six feet away from the ride going up and down and round and round. I remember the horses on the ride because I was wishing I could sit on one and have a ride, when I was suddenly violently dragged away by my hair, screamed at and slapped around the face from left to right until I felt sick and giddy.

That's what I remember about that day at Whipsnade Zoo. I've tried but I remember nothing else, only that part of the day. I had only been there ten minutes when that happened. I do remember wanting to go home to someone that loved me, my mom.

17. DINNERS – ONE DAY ONLY

During my first week at school I heard other children saying how much they enjoyed the dinners and puddings they had there, the thought of puddings made me want school dinners. The boy who became my friend stayed for school dinners and told me all about them, his name was Michael Luckman, we were never apart. Michael never once made any comment on my appearance but sadly he died of Leukaemia at the tender age of 14, I think of him even to this day. We were in the junior football team together, we won the league in 1955, he is standing next to me on the photograph and you will see 1955 written on the ball.

My mom had to plead and beg the headmistress to let me stay for school dinners because Mom didn't work and both parents had to be at work, so I wasn't really allowed to stay for school dinners. Only certain poor children got free meals, my mom paid for that week. I heard girls taking the mick out of the children who had free dinners saying, "Our moms have to pay so why should you get them free, your parents are scroungers." Children can be so hurtful.

So, for my first school dinner I was a very excited, all I could think about were those puddings. We had to line up in the corridor to go into the hall where all the table and chairs were placed out in two rows. As I stood in the queue the girls were saying to me, "You can't stand by me", "Don't touch me, stand away." So I moved, then I was told by another girl, "I don't want you by me." Even the boys started pushing me around, I started at the front of the queue and I ended up at the back. In we went in single file holding the trays as we marched in. Every time I went to sit down, I was told, "You can't sit by me." I was feeling very low and very much alone by this time. The teacher must have seen what was going on, she told me to "sit there" pointing to a vacant chair and I sat opposite the cruellest girl I have ever known who said, "Why did she put you opposite me? I told you in the queue I don't want you by me and don't look at me while I am eating my dinner," she made me feel terrible. "You sit somewhere else tomorrow, I don't want you looking at me."

We had fish for dinner and on the table was a bottle of parsley sauce, I didn't know what it was, then I saw a boy pick the same type of bottle up on the next table so I thought it must be okay to put it on my dinner. I picked up the bottle that was by me and shook it hard just like the brown sauce we had at home, I always had to shake it hard to get the sauce out and thought this sauce must be the same. Well, it smothered my dinner, I was horrified! I tried it but I didn't like it. The girl opposite me started on me again, "I bet you never have sauce in your house, bet your parents can't afford it, you only put that much sauce on because you are a pig! Now you can't eat it. Miss! Miss!" She shouted to the teacher, "He has put lots of sauce on his dinner now he is not eating it." The teacher, I remember, was very kind she said "never mind" to me and walked away. That horrible girl kept saying, "Pig, pig. Anyway you shouldn't be here your mom doesn't work I bet you haven't paid for it like my mom paid for me, pig." I never said a word to that girl all through dinner. I tried to eat it but found I didn't like it, the sauce that is, so I didn't have any dinner. We had apple pie and custard for dessert. The girl opposite said, "I see you have eaten all that and you ate it quick, you pig. I bet you never get puddings at home."

The reason I shook the parsley sauce bottle the way I did, I explained to the teacher, was because at home we always had to shake the brown sauce like that, with a calming hand on my shoulder she said, "it's all right David." The last words I remember that horrid girl saying to me were, "Anyway you shouldn't be here your parents don't look after you." She was so cruel, I had tears in my eyes. When you stayed for school dinners you weren't allowed to leave the school premises so I sat in the corner of the playground to stay away from that girl even then I saw her pointing to me as she was talking to some other girls.

When I went home that evening from school, I told my mom I wasn't staying for school dinners anymore. She went mad at me, saying, "After all the pleading and begging I did to your headmistress and now you don't want to stay for dinners anymore and I paid for the whole week." "I don't like the school dinners," I said, I never told her the real truth. The truth was I was too afraid to sit opposite that cruel girl and be tormented. That was my first and last school dinner. That girl was right about the pudding, we rarely got them at home, well not on a weekday sometimes we did on a Sunday. I wonder what she is like now? I bet she doesn't remember how cruel she was. I would like to think she does remember and regrets what a horrible little girl she was.

18. AN APPLE A DAY

When I started school the second teacher I had was called Miss Pitt, I loved her and I was in her class till I went into the juniors. One day while she was telling us something she suddenly said, "David, come here." I remember this moment so well. When I got to her desk she opened the drawer, well it was more a lid than a draw, took out an apple which she held out to me and said, "Here is an apple for you." She placed it in my hand and started to say "but…" the apple went straight into my mouth that fast, I think she was going to say, "don't eat it until playtime. Oh, all right David go and sit down and eat it as quick as you can." I wonder if any of the other children were questioning why they never got an apple, if it had been me seeing another child being given an apple, I would have thought why can't I have one?

What a wonderful lady, I was so thin, poorly dressed and I think maybe I was malnourished. Every day that very thoughtful lady brought me an apple and she would say, "I'm going to give you an apple at playtime," which she did. Thank you Miss Pitt and God bless you, wherever you are.

My teacher Miss Pitt, giving me an apple.

19. MY FIRST TRAM RIDE

My first tram ride was to the Lickey Hills, this I remember very well, well after my wife jogged my memory, it's funny the things that trigger your memory. I was five years old, before my younger brother John was born, and Mom took me and my three sisters Janet, Doreen and Kathleen to the Lickey Hills on a tram. We travelled on a number 14 bus from Audley Road, Glebe Farm in Stechford into Birmingham city centre. I can remember getting off the bus in the Old Square, from there we walked through the Minories which fascinated me because the road had been laid with rubber blocks. We walked under Lewis's bridge across Bull Street along Temple Row until we reached St Philip's cathedral (this was the cathedral I attended for my school leavers' service at the age of fifteen). We crossed over the churchyard leading us to Colmore Row and walked along the busy road to the end. Across the road on the left-hand side stood the Post Office with, what to me, seemed a very large revolving door. On the left of this building was Hill Street, which was quite a steep hill going down crossing over the railway bridge, the walls were much too high to see over but at least I could smell and hear the trains. At the bottom of the hill we turned into Navigation Street and to my amazement a wonderful sight to see, all the trams lined up with queues of people waiting to get on, what seemed to me at that time hundreds of people.

I had never been on a train at that time but even at the tender age of five I loved trains, the clickety-clack sound they made on the rails. Me and my new friend Trevor went to Stechford railway station to watch the trains go by, we were allowed to roam all over the place and at such a young age, so going on a tram seemed to me like going on a train. Once I was on the tram, I was so excited, the swaying and the clickety-clack were just a dream to me. I can still see those polished wooden benches with the reversible back rests. I was sitting by the window looking at the world going by, I was so happy I was whistling. My sister Kathleen who was sitting on the other side of the tram opposite me shouted to me, "David, for God's sake shut up!" Mom said to her, "Oh leave him alone, he's just happy." So I stopped whistling, I bet to the delight of the other passengers.

We arrived at the terminus which was situated at the bottom of the Lickey Hills, well almost. I remember there were what seemed like a thousand steps to go up, I ran up those steps in my excitement to see what was at the top, it was all trees. Mom, being a large lady, struggled to climb those steps I bet they are still there. Mom took sandwiches and a bottle of pop and there was a steep bank, nothing on it just grass. I thought I would roll down the hill but I went much faster than I thought I would, it made me very giddy and scared if I'm honest. As I stood up, I fell over, my sense of balance was all over the place.

When I finally regained my senses, I went exploring. I remember thinking, I'm going to be an explorer, as boys do. I strayed further away from my mom than I should have, when I suddenly realised I was lost. I was starting to quietly panic and how long I was away from my family I'm not sure, it most probably was only a few minutes. I wandered around aimlessly looking for them, then to my delight I saw them through the bushes sitting on a bench eating sandwiches and drinking pop. I waited a couple of minutes to calm myself down then I slowly walked up to them and said, "I've been exploring. Can I have a sandwich please, I'm hungry."

"I'll give you sandwich my lad, I've been worried to death," Mom said sternly.

"Why?" I asked calmly trying to act like I didn't know.

"Right, you stay where I can see you."

"Okay, mom," I replied. No way was I going to explore anymore, I was afraid of getting lost again. So, I played with my sisters until Mom shouted, "Come on you lot we are going back now!" Yeah, I thought, back on that tram I was overjoyed. To me that was the best part of the day out riding on that tram, it's a shame that young people can't experience riding round the cities on a tram the same as the ones I rode on.

20. IRON HORSE

I've already mentioned Barry, who lived next door, he was five years older than me. He loved the small hours of the morning and boy could he talk, 'he could talk the leg off an iron pot' as the saying goes and no matter how tired I became, he just would not go home. I made friends with Barry as soon as I started to walk, we sort of hit it off from day one. I kept in touch with Barry until the day he died, which was in 2009, and was a sad loss of a very dear friend.

Looking back to his and my childhood, when I was only six years old, he took me to a place called Coleshill. As I've mentioned he and his family loved fishing and the thing I remember about that day and the reason I remember it so well was there were stepping stones going across the river, one was very green with moss. The river was quite shallow where the stepping stones were, I remember his very words to me, "Mind how you step on this stone, it's very slippy," he said pointing to the stone. Not taking a lot of notice and thinking I knew best, I jumped onto that stone, yes jumped. Of course I slipped and fell in, Barry looked at me and laughed, he said "I told you it was slippy."

To a skinny six-year-old the water seemed to be deep, it came past my waist. Barry waded in, picked me up and carried me to the bank. We started to walk across the field to head home, with me still dripping wet, when Barry saw an LMS railway three-wheeler lorry. He ran very quickly to the gate and waved like mad with his coat, talk about luck or coincidence, it turned out it was Barry's dad. He had worked on the railways from a boy, his depot was in Nechells in Rupert Street, Birmingham. Barry shouted "Come on, Dave, it's my dad!" Barry's dad looked at me and smiled, he never laughed but he could see I was distressed because I was soaking wet. "And what happened to you, young man?" he asked as if he didn't know.

"I fell into the river," I replied.

"Come on, young fella," he said, "I will take you home in my Iron Horse."

"Iron Horse?" I asked.

"Yes, David that's what they call these lorries," he said, "you sit on the cowling, you'll get dry on there."

I got lovely and warm sitting on that cowling, it was a cover that fitted over the engine. I loved that lorry, I thought to myself, I'm going to drive one of these when I grow up. When I did grow up, I passed my test on those Iron Horses, I really loved driving them and would you believe it, I worked alongside Barry's dad! When I called him by his surname, which I had done from birth, he said "David, you're an adult now call me Bunny." Calling him by his first name was very strange to me because I was brought up to say Mr and Mrs, if I didn't, my mom would clout me round the ear. So it was always by their surname which I still do to this day.

By the way, that wasn't the last time I went into the river while I was growing up, it happened a few times. That first soaking I got was at the bottom of a hill in Coleshill called Maxstoke Lane, the river is known as the Blythe. I spent many a happy hour over the following years in that same field, the difference was, I had swimming trunks on.

Incidentally the correct name for the three-wheel Iron Horse is Scammel Scarab. I have written a book entitled *Lick 'Em On I'm Off* it's about my working adult life and there is a chapter in my book showing a picture of me with one of those iron horses.

21. TWO BIRTHDAY CARDS

I've sat and thought very hard about this, did I ever get a present for my birthday? I cannot bring to mind any. I did get a windjammer, as they were called at that time, just before my ninth birthday. I felt really smart and very warm, well, I could fasten it up and I suppose that could be classed as a present. It was a wonderful gift and I loved it, it was brown and zipped right up to the neck. I was allowed to go outside wearing my new coat to show it to Trevor, but then I was told I must go back inside and take it off.

Trevor was so jealous, as I was showing him my windjammer I didn't see him pick up a handful of dirt, well more like dust really. As we were talking, he threw the dirt over my new coat and ran off like the wind into his house. I ran after him, knocked on his back door and his mom came and said, "Trevor told me to tell you he doesn't feel well, he is not playing out today." We laughed about it the next day, we never fell out but I did it to him the first chance I had which was a long, long time after that little episode.

I wasn't allowed to wear that windjammer again until my brother got married in the December of that year and I wore that coat for his wedding. Maybe that's why I got the new coat for my birthday and wasn't allowed to play out in it till after the wedding. Mom bought it from Evans the club man, he called every Saturday afternoon for money as it was paid for weekly.

One year I remember when it was my birthday, I was nine years old, Trevor's mom (my mom's best friend Lizzie) gave me a postcard birthday card, that's the type we used to get in those days. She put 2/- (two shillings) in with the card, the first and last time that happened. Some years I got two cards – one off my mom and one from Trevor's mom. I never, as far as I can remember, got more than two cards it just never happened. Nor in all my young days did I ever have a birthday cake or a party. Well, better I ate food than have a party, a toy car or a game – my mom's words.

22. MY FIRST CAR RIDE

My first car accident was in 1950, when cars owned by the working classes were few and far between. How it came about was my two eldest brothers were converting a fish and chip van into a caravanette. All this took place on an old farm, not long before it was demolished, only a couple of miles from where I lived. The chip van was equipped with all its fryers still in situ and all the fat still in it, the smell of old grease and chip fat was horrible. Anyway, I was given a scraper and told to get as much fat as I could off the walls. "Don't get dirty!" was my eldest brother's command. I ask you, with fat and grease everywhere how could I not get grease on me? I obeyed his wish, well I tried to. Yes, I got grease and fat on me. "Leave that now," he said, "it's okay." So very quickly I dropped the scraper.

I stood and watched him sawing slots in a piece of 2x2 inch timber. I wanted to do that too and picked up a saw and started to saw one of the slots he had been sawing. I will soon get through this, I thought, and he will be pleased with me (secretly I thought he would give me some money for helping him – wrong). Suddenly there was a deafening shout of, "Don't cut through that, put the saw down!" My nerves took an Olympic high jump. What he explained, when he came back down to earth, was when a piece has many slots cut in it you can bend it, he pointed to the round front of an old caravan, "that's what these two pieces of wood will do, form a round front over the driver's cab."

My dad came to see how they were doing, he was very impressed with them. A few minutes after Dad arrived my eldest brother Donald's friend George turned up, he lived across the road from our house. George arrived in a brand-new bright shiny black car, he had only had it a week, the smell of the leather interior is something I shall never forget. A few minutes later my brothers decided to pack up and go home, George said, "Come on, I'll give you a lift in my new car."

I was very excited, I had never been in a car before! We drove out of the farm gate, then turned right and it felt like we were doing a thousand miles an hour, well it was fast. I remember the words my dad said to me, "Hang on to your hat, son, this is the fastest you will ever go down this road." I'm not wearing a hat, I was thinking, I wonder why he thinks I'm wearing a hat? (okay I'm not the brightest pin in the box). We were flying, we came to the railway bridge (which has since has been widened) and we started to climb to reach the brow of the bridge. There wasn't any way of seeing if there were any other vehicles coming over the bridge on the other side. Just as we reached the brow, George was too far over to the right and we slammed straight into an oncoming car, it folded up like cardboard.

The poor man sat with a glazed look on his face, his car was absolutely smashed up. George had pushed the car right up against the bridge wall so the man could not get out of any of the doors. My dad told me to go home and tell Mom he would be late home for dinner, I ran like the wind non-stop until I reached home, puffing and panting for breath. I blurted out, "We

Scraping by. The first car accident I was in.

*The bridge where my first car accident
took place in Church Road, Stechford.*

The bridge from the other side of Church Road.

have been in a car smash, Mom. It's all smashed up!" Poor Mom went white and staggered to her chair, she sat down with tears streaming down her face. She said, "Oh my god!" Mom thought that my dad and brothers had all been smashed up and were all in hospital. "Where are they? Where are they?" she kept saying. I was confused, I couldn't understand why she was so upset. She stood up and started running round the room like a headless chicken. "Oh," I said calmly, "I forgot to tell you, Dad said he would be a little late home for dinner." Once again she staggered to the chair, nerves all shot. With a stare she says to me, "You silly little bugger, I thought your dad and brothers had been seriously injured." I replied, "No, the car's been smashed up not the men, there's nothing wrong with them they're okay."

I learned in later years, from my brother Donald, that even though it was George's fault the insurance company would not pay out, both men blamed each other for the accident. It turned out that the other poor man had just repaired his engine and was out testing it, he had no tax.

I remember I was not frightened or shaken at all, I was very calm. That was my first car accident.

23. STREAMERS

Suches was a hardware shop that sold paraffin, crockery, statues, glass, wood, brooms, mops, nails, screws and even wallpaper. They also sold balls of chalk and blue cubes that you mixed with the chalk, Mom said it made the white look whiter when blue was mixed in with the chalk. She used it to whitewash the coalhouse but the trouble was when you rubbed against the walls, chalk came off on your clothes.

Suches was at the end of a row of shops next to the pub known as the Glebe Farm, in later years it was changed to the Cock and Bull. Across the road was a shop called Stanley James where my mom bought linoleum, we always called it lino, it was the cheapest form of floor covering you could get at that time. It looked beautiful when first laid down with bright vibrant colours, but after a very short time if it carried a lot of traffic the pattern soon wore off. My mom always fitted the lino, never my dad. It was a huge fire hazard, it burnt fiercely.

Mom even did all the painting and decorating in our house, she was brilliant at wallpaper hanging, she bought the paper from Suches. Back in the 1940s the edge was left on the wallpaper, but for a small fee the paper was put on a machine and rolled onto a long roller then back again, it cut through the edging so when the roll was tapped on the table the cut edge would fall off. When Mom couldn't afford to pay the extra money to have the rolls trimmed, she would sit for what seemed like hours and cut off the edge with a pair of scissors. I also saw Mom leave the edge on, but when put on the wall and overlapped, a bulge from top to bottom of the edge could be seen on every strip. It didn't look too bad but not the job really, I went to many houses and saw paper hung like that in fact I helped my mom to hang paper like that.

When I was about seven or eight, after she had cut off the edge, I would ask if I could have the edges to play with, she always said no but with a lot of nagging she would give in. I was told, "Don't throw them in the horse road, put them in the dustbin when you have finished playing with them." But after me and my friends had thrown them at each other and had lots of fun I got fed up rolling them up so as you can imagine, yes, I left those streamers scattered all over the road. I was told to get the cane from the coal house, it was too late to say sorry, three whacks across the bum so I ended up picking it all up after all and binning it. When Mom folded her arms and said to do it, you did it or get the cane from the coalhouse. Children never learn, do they? Well, I never did, that's for sure.

24. GROWING ANOTHER HEAD

Before I started school at the age of five, I had a bubble grow out of the right side of my head between my ear and eye, you could see the blood pumping round it. I was taken to the Children's Hospital in Birmingham and when the doctor looked at it, he was puzzled. He didn't know what it was or why it had happened. I heard him say to my mother, "I won't bandage it, let the air get to it, it looks like an artery that has grown out of his head." He took Mom to one side, he must have thought I was deaf, and in a low voice I heard him say, "Whatever happens, Mother, he must not make it bleed or he could bleed to death." Well, I was frightened to death!

Those words scared the life out of me, as a young child they would wouldn't they? After that day I did make it bleed and spurt out, I had my own waterfall only mine was in blood. It happened many times and every time I would run to my mom saying, "Mom, it's bleeding am I going to die? Am I going to die?" At the same time crying my eyes out. I used to turn over in bed and make it bleed and the pillow used to be covered in blood. The worst time it bled (and boy did it bleed) I was play fighting with my cousin who lived with us at the time (he was the one that took me on the bus when I broke my leg). He suddenly said to me, "You're bleeding." I went to my mom screaming and again saying, "Am I going to die? Am I am going to die?" She ran me into the kitchen picked me up and put my head under the tap, she just kept dabbing it with piece of rag, as the water was cascading over my head the rag got soaked in blood it was everywhere. My mom was crying while she was doing it. It seemed a long time being done but it did stop eventually. That was the most worrying time of my young life. But eventually it did go away, it started to go down. The doctor at the Children's Hospital was putting some sort of ointment on it to slowly freeze it, so my mom told me years later when I was in my teens.

When playing with my friends once, they were surprised to see blood pumping from it after I headed the ball. Many years later my mom said that she was worried to death and thought she was going to lose me every time it bled, it was such an ordeal for her because her life was hard enough.

25. ICED GEMS

My mom was known by all the local shopkeepers in our area because she used their shops all through the war and people got preferential treatment if they used the same shops. I remember her going into Wrenson's after the war and asking for a quarter of a pound of iced gems, those little round biscuits with a dab of icing sugar in the middle. "Sorry you are not one of my regular customers," said Mr Oakley, the manager. I believe things were still on rationing because of the sugar shortage that was still on then. My mom wasn't very happy to hear him say that to her, so she told him a few home truths, I remember I got a little worried because of the way he raised his voice to her. Mom's friend Winnie (my friend Johnny's mom) used Wrenson's all the time so she went in and bought iced gems for my mom. Mr Oakley asked Winnie, "Are you buying these for her?" She replied, "I'm buying them for myself and it's none of your business what I buy or who for!"

When mom was hard up, she used to make me go to Holidays, the local butcher, she had used this butcher all through the war and I used to have to go and ask for two pence worth of bones for the dog, he knew we didn't have a dog. He would go to the back of his shop and gave me lots of bones wrapped in newspaper, he always said, "Tell Dora, I mean your mom, they haven't been on the floor and there is quite a lot of meat still on the bone." Mom made a stew with them and made it last for three or four days.

26. PEG RUGS

When Trevor and I were collecting rags from all the houses around our area to make money, my mom saw us going through the rags and asked if we had any coats in the sacks. There were two coats in one of the sacks so we gave them to her. She washed and dried them, then I helped Mom to cut them up into long strips about one inch wide by six inches long, so she could make peg rugs. The lengths of material were looped through a piece of canvas and the different colours of the material were sometimes made into a pattern.

It took my mom and me some time to make a peg rug but I really enjoyed making it with her and my sisters, we loved sitting on it in front of the fire. Mom lined the back of the rug with oddments of materials when it was placed in front of the fire it was a joy for me to sit on it, it felt soft and very cosy.

It would have been nice to have one at the side of my bed it would have made such a difference in the winter months to stand on the rug instead of the icy cold lino. I was sitting on the one by the fire place one day when I saw loads of silver things, I asked Mom what they were she called them silver fish. I used to watch them running around if I moved, they would vanish very quickly. Mom also told me those silver fish lived in the hot fire ashes, I thought no way, they would get burnt. When I was asked to empty the ashes next morning, I did see those silver fish in amongst all that dust and those ashes were still hot.

I was sometimes told to put the peg rug on the line and beat it with the yard broom, the dust that used to come out of it was from the ashes from the coal fire and I ended up all grey from the ash dust.

Those rugs looked good when down and lasted a very long time. I wonder what people would think these days if they went into a friend's house and saw peg rugs? It wouldn't happen these days, we are all spoiled are we not.

27. BIRMINGHAM POST AND MAIL

In my first year at the junior school, as I walked into the class room as playtime finished, I noticed the teacher staring at me. She called out to me to go to her and I was thinking what have I done wrong? I went to the desk where she was sitting writing a letter which she folded and handed to me saying, "Take this letter and give it to your mother." "Okay Miss," I said. I went to sit down, I was thinking she was complaining about me to my mom. I will rip it up, I thought, I couldn't read so ripping it up was the only solution. "No David," she said, "take it home to your mom now." "What, leave school now Miss?" "Yes, go straight home now."

I think it was about 11am. Well, getting out of school I didn't need telling twice! My feet went so fast through the playground I nearly fell over, I had to run fast in case the teacher changed her mind. My mom's face when I walked in, and in the rush to get out of school I had forgotten to rip up the letter, "What are you doing out of school?" "My teacher said I could leave school and give you this letter." Well Mom was so delighted when she read the letter, she rushed into the hall to get her coat and said, "Come on quick, we can get there in time." We ran up the road, Mom being a large lady, was really puffing and blowing with beads of sweat on her brow. We were just in time as the bus had just stopped at the bus stop, Mom was shouting "Hold it miss!" to the conductress. We got on the bus, "Where are we going?" I kept asking. "Shh," she said. I didn't know what was happening. We got off the bus in the Old Square in Birmingham city centre. We were really rushing and I hadn't a clue what was going on.

We ended up in a building with loads of boots and shoes everywhere and that smell you get when in a shoe shop, but this smell was different from a shoe shop smell you get today of course, it was leather then. I never forgot that smell. My mom handed the letter to the man (why did grown-ups look so stern in those says?). Mom sat me down, took off my holy pumps and socks (my footwear in those days was very religious!), it was winter and I remember because my feet were wet.

The man handed Mom a lovely pair of socks and as he turned away she got out her handkerchief to dry my feet with, then put the socks on me. They were grey and so was the pattern round the top, they felt so thick and warm, then to my surprise the man was trying boots on me. No these are no good, I heard him saying to himself, he went away and I was horrified. "Mom, I can make them fit," I said to her. "It's all right, son he is getting a bigger pair for you." Boy was I relived, he tried two different sizes on me before saying, "Yes, these are alright." I asked, "Can I keep them on?"

"Of course you can, son," the man said as he patted me on the head. "Yes," said Mom at the same time she thanked the man and out we went.

Wow, can you imagine not having to tuck your sock under your foot to put some space between your foot and the pavement because of the holes in your pumps and not having a soaking wet foot? I used to put cardboard in my pumps when the sock was so worn out and there wasn't enough material left to tuck under my foot but when cardboard got wet it made my feet wetter plus it went all soggy and fell apart. When the weather was good the pavement rubbed it away to nothing in minutes.

I walked out of that building with warm feet and legs but best of all I was walking with dry feet in the rain. I was so happy. I remember that day very well it felt good. I now know the letter my teacher gave to me was for a free pair of boots and socks from that wonderful establishment known as the *Birmingham Post and Mail*. I believe they are also referred to as Daily Mail Boots. It turned out that a lot of children at school knew if you had your free boots and socks, but if you didn't wear the socks they couldn't tell where the boots came from. I believe the girls' shoes had eyelets in the sides of the shoe, which let other children know where the shoes had come from and that they were free shoes.

Off to school the next day I was feeling very warm and proud of my new boots when two boys came up to me and very loudly said, "Free boots because your parents can't buy you any?" I answered with, "I had these yesterday my mom bought them for me." "No, she didn't you only get those socks when your parents have no money and you get them from the Birmingham Post and Mail, you are a scruffy scrounger, your parents don't look after you," they teased. I suffered many more comments from a lot of boys but more horrible comments from the girls. Well at least my feet were warm and dry and the teasing, ridicule and torment stopped after a couple of days. One morning I heard another boy getting the same treatment from the boys and girls that I had got from them the week before. Children were so cruel especially the ones that were brought up in better living conditions than the boy or girl they were tormenting.

28. WHITE MICE

The old market hall in Birmingham city centre had large steps leading up into, what to me looked like, a massive space with lots of traders selling so many different types of goods. It was just like Aladdin's cave with all the traders shouting at the same time trying to attract the attention of the people as they passed their stalls. This shell of a building, with arches in the walls every few feet that were once windows, made me walk round in awe of the place and I seem to remember two big pillars either side of the steps at the entrance.

I went on a Saturday with my friend Trevor and I bought a little white mouse from there for 6d (sixpence). But not being able to tell the difference between male and females I ended up with twenty-three white mice! I gave them to many of my friends that wanted to keep mice, free of charge.

When I first started to collect mice, I said to the man selling them, "Mister, can I have that one?" He picked up the wrong mouse so I said, "Not that one, that one." He picked one up and with a deep breath, a puff and a few choice words he said, "Look, son do you want this mouse or don't you. I ain't got all day and they are all the bloody same, do you want it?" "Yes please, Mister," I said with a trembling voice. He placed the mouse in a box and I gave him my sixpence. Feeling very pleased with my new mouse, I hurried to the bus stop and I got on the number 14 bus to go home. When on the bus upstairs, I thought I would take a peep at my new little friend. I didn't know mice were so fast and as soon as it saw the chink of light it shot out of the box, ran up my arm and across my shoulders. I just managed to grab its tail, it didn't like that because it bit my finger and drew blood, so I threw him back in the box as quick as he came out. I won't do that again, I thought.

Back home Barry from next door gave me all the equipment and the mouse box, it was like Christmas come early, it had a sliding glass lid inside a well-made nesting box, I felt so proud of my box. Bowls for food and a bottle clipped to the side for water. In went the mouse, I felt so good I kept looking at it all through the day. My mom said I couldn't keep it in the house so it stayed in the back yard. I covered it over with a waterproof canvas to keep it warm.

All was well for a few weeks but one afternoon Barry's cat had slid back the glass lid and got the mouse out before I could get there, it was so badly cut I was in tears. I called Robert, the neighbour who lived in the house joining my house, I asked "Rob can you help?" "It's suffering, Dave," he said. "I can't kill it, Rob," I said. "I'll do it for you," he said and threw it hard onto the concrete floor, "it's dead now," he said. I buried it in the garden and made a little cross for it.

More errands to run and a couple of weeks later I bought another white mouse, I didn't open the box until I reached home, I had learned my lesson and this time I put half of a house brick on top of the box so the cat couldn't slide the glass. A week later I bought another one just to give my first one a friend and as I was cleaning them out two weeks later, to my surprise there were six babies (talk about rabbits!). After cleaning them out I forgot to put the house brick back on the glass and the cat killed them, he took them one at a time to his garden next door they were scattered all over the lawn, he killed all eight mice.

I just sat looking at all those baby mice lying on the grass next door and that was the end of me keeping pets. I shouted to Robert over the back fence, "Rob, do you want this mouse box?"

"Yes please, Dave," he said so I gave him every item plus some items I had bought.

"Why are you getting rid of them, Dave?"

"It's the second time that cat has killed my mice, he won't kill any more of my mice because I won't have any for him to kill!"

29. SHARE NUMBER

The Co-operative Society (Co-op), now that was the shop that really fascinated me to the point where my imagination ran riot. My mom sent me to the Co-op many times over the years and I went with her to buy items from that store. My mom would say, "Don't forget to give my share number," that number is burned into my brain, 77467 it rolls off the tongue like poetry. When I got married, I could never remember our Co-op number, much to the annoyance of my wife, I gave my mom's number.

I remember those wires that went from the counter to the cash office upstairs, where there were two ladies that could be seen through big glass windows. The ladies serving on the shop floor weren't allowed to handle the cash in those days (it's hard to imagine that now, isn't it?) so they wrote down the cost of the groceries that had been purchased on a slip with the customer's name on it and what money was given. The slip was then placed in the cylinder, which to me looked like a bomb, with the money, the cylinder's lid was on a wire (I think that's how it went, my memory is fading a little!). The next operation really got my attention, after the lady had fixed it to the wire, she pulled on a wire with a wooden handle attached to it, the bomb would travel what seemed very fast to me, it went upwards along the ceiling and straight into the cash office, they would sort out what change was needed then send it back to the ladies serving on the shop floor, with the slip and the change. They would call out the name of the person to give them their change, always the surname never by their Christian name, if by this time they were half way through serving another customer one had to wait for the change till they had finished serving that customer. I don't think that system would work these days everyone seems to be in so much of a rush don't they? It's a shame they didn't leave that system in the shop, people would go in just to look at it and of course spend while they were in there.

My mom saved up the dividend until Christmas if she could, which wasn't very often, as at that time of her life things were very hard. That dividend book was a life saver at times, I went with my mom a few times to get the money out. We went to the main Co-op store in Birmingham city centre, which I believe was the only place Mom could go to for the divi (dividend), she always called it the divi. I remember a couple of times she only got one shilling and sixpence 1/6d and was very glad to have it I might add, times were very hard for Mom in those days.

The dividend book was black with hard covers and quite large. I seem to remember all entries in the book were done by hand when Mom did a withdrawal. She told me if you want quality, shop at the Co-op. They were dearer than most other shops, so Mom rarely bought household goods from the Co-op, she had to settle for cheaper goods from other stores. As the old saying goes if you have only one shilling you can't spend two, as I've already mentioned, my mom said that to me quite a few times through my life. Another saying she very often said was don't worry, you die if you worry, you will die even if you don't so no point in worrying. She said that to my wife one day when she was worrying about paying the rent because she was short of money and would you believe it, it changed how she thought about things from that day on.

30. SATURDAY PAY OUT

An occurrence that happened every Saturday morning, wasn't anything to do with me directly, indirectly maybe. Mom could not go out on a Saturday morning, that's the time when what we called club men came (and club women) in the main though it was men. Families where I was brought up, lived on the 'glad and sorry' so called because whatever you bought off those club men you paid a small amount of money for every week until you had paid back all the cost of the item plus interest. That's why it was called the glad and sorry, glad to have it, sorry to have to pay for it.

Mom could only survive this way as most people did in those days. Mom had shoes, coats, bed linen and kitchen utensils, even paraffin heaters. Yes, if you were willing to pay weekly those club people were only too happy to sell it to you so you owed them that much money, they kept you in debt for years and they could keep making profit off you. As the amount came down to almost nil this worried them so they would try very hard to tempt you to buy more items off them, they would even make believe they would reduce any item for you because you were a good valued customer but of course it was all over-priced to start with. Well, on the other hand if those firms had not been around most people would never been able to buy anything, it was no way to live but it was then the only way for my family.

Every Saturday we had Evans, S and U, Sloanes, the coalman and the milkman, all calling for some money. To help Mom make her few pennies go further she would say to one of them, "I can't pay you this week." Boy did they moan. She would say to another one, "I can only pay you 3d (three pence)."

"Is that all, Mrs Prosser? It's not enough you know," they would say. I used to like the look on their faces when Mom would say to them, "Okay, if you don't want it, I will give it to Evans then."

"No, I'll take it," they always answered. Mom did this balancing act with the few pennies she had for years; if she paid 2d or 3d to one, whichever one she missed she would give them double the week after if she could afford it and not pay the ones she gave a few pennies to the week before, and some weeks they were all given nothing at all. I saw my mom in tears over club men pushing for money out of her. Mom always robbed Peter to pay Paul as the saying goes (the good old days, eh!), well they were the good old days for me but not for people like my mom who were trying to survive. Those clubmen were crooks, they always over charged for the goods they were pushing to the poor.

31. FARES PLEASE

My sisters and me used to put the four dining room chairs together in a row, pretending it was a bus, and we would take it in turns to be the driver and the conductor. We did this many times in our young lives. My younger brother John was in his very early years at this time so my sister Doreen would sit him on her lap and make the engine noise to him and rock about to give the feel of the moving bus. My sister Janet would also do this for him. Of course, as the years went by, he sat on the chairs and made his own noises like an engine, as I did.

Sometimes, but not very often actually it was quite rare, my mom would go with Trevor's mom Lizzie to have a quiet drink for an hour. As the saying goes, while the cat's away the mice will play, that is so true. Our favourite game when no parents were around was to get a pillow and a blanket from the bed, put the blanket over the top stair, sit on the pillow and be pulled down the stairs (no carpet in those days only lino). Well, it was great fun for us screaming and shouting, we drove our neighbours to the edge of despair, it must have been a nightmare to live next door to us. The next-door neighbour used to come round and be pulling his hair out.

One particular evening we were playing tig and tag – you know, keep your feet off the ground, if touched by the one that's on when your feet were on the ground it was your turn to be on. The only difference this time we were doing it in the house running up and down the stairs, out the front door round the back through the back door shouting and I suppose making quite a lot of noise. My mom came in, shouted and told us to play more quietly. Children play quietly? Not us lot, that's for sure, but because Mom was home we had to calm it down a little. My mom, bless her, liked to see her children playing, she always said when she could see her children playing she knew we were happy.

The next-door neighbour came round and banged on the door, my cheeky sister Doreen opened the door, the poor neighbour was so annoyed he said, "I'm really fed up with you lot." My sister was smirking at him. He said, "You'll smirk on the other side of your face in a minute," then he said, "I suppose your mother is in the bloody pub again." My mom popped her head around the living room door and replied, "No she bloody well isn't!" A few words were exchanged! Mom's favourite saying then was "got to play don't they, can't stop kids playing." Well, no way would I like to have lived next door to a family as noisy as we were.

Many years later when talking about it to my mom (the years fade the memories for some people) I think she said, "You weren't that bad." Boy, if we weren't I would hate to live by children that were only half as bad as we were. "We were very noisy, Mom!" I said to her. But I must agree with you, Mom, when children are playing they are happy, your children most certainly were.

32. PLAYING GAMES
WITH BROTHER JOHN

We really did drive the next-door neighbours mad. As we lived in a semi-detached house the floors were joined through the walls, so every time we jumped on the floorboards it sounded like we were in their house. They had four children two grown up lads and two young children a boy and a girl, we never heard a peep out of them.

As children do, my youngest brother John and I were playing tig around all three bedrooms running, screaming, shouting, jumping all over the beds and having a jolly good time. We hadn't any carpets in our house, so every time we jumped off the bed onto the floor, well it sounded like thunder. As we were running from one room to the next, John still trying to tig me, I ran from Mom's room, to the little bedroom across the landing with John close behind me. I swung the door to the closed position and John's big toe went under the door, his scream was deafening! It made a terrible mess of his big toe and he was taken to hospital.

I got a good hiding, well deserved I suppose, but we were only playing. He suffered for a long time after with that toe, in fact, I took him some time ago to have that toenail off at the foot clinic (at the Swan, Yardley) maybe because of that accident all those years ago his nail was never the same. We were young lads just playing and enjoying life.

33. "LONESOME"

I came home from school one afternoon when I heard sounds coming from the living room, I ran in very excited. I looked in the cupboard at the side of the fireplace and to my surprise there were a dozen chicks all cuddled together, little balls of yellow fluff. I was so excited, Mom told me my eldest brother Donald had brought them home, where from I have no idea. He may have got them from the rag and bone man, they had a horse and cart in those days and you could get chicks from them by giving them old rags, the man used go through them to make sure the clothes or rags were clean. Mind you for a dozen chicks he would have wanted a good sack full of old clothes.

As a child does, I kept picking the chicks up and unfortunately one by one they died, after only a very short time only one remained Mom named it Lonesome. It grew big and as it was growing up, I noticed that every time I went by it pecked me, it pecked me even when I walked into the room and it was the same with my sisters. I played with Lonesome a lot while it was growing, well one could say I tormented it, I suppose it must have been getting its own back. Mom was the only one that could do anything with it, it never did peck her.

I couldn't go into the backyard without that chicken flying at me, I always ended up climbing up the line post screaming, "Mom, Mom! The chicken is pecking me!" She would open the back door and shout, "Get in that bloody pen now." My eldest brother had built the pen and the chicken would stop dead in its tracks, its head would go down as it looked at Mom, "I won't tell you again, get in that pen." It jumped down the two steps and very slowly it walked into the pen. "I hate that bird," I would say. Mom always said, "It's all right. You must be tormenting it."

Every day I would shout through the letterbox, "Mom, is the chicken out?" Sometimes she didn't answer me, another time she said, "It's locked up," when it wasn't. I would walk into the backyard and that silly bird would either chase me up the line post or into the outside loo. If it was the loo, it walked up and down outside the door, there was a gap under the toilet door and it would pop its head in the gap every now and again making a terrible noise to see if I was still there. I used to try and kick it but it was always too quick for me. I would be shouting at the top of my voice for ages calling, "Mom!" When she finally came and locked the chicken up, she would smile and say, "I forgot I had let it out."

Every time I wanted to go in the backyard, I would rattle the gate and shout, "I'm coming in!" Nothing, all quiet. Good, it's locked up, I thought, in I go. Just as I'm was about to open the back door out would fly the chicken from the side of the pen making a terrible noise, pecking me all the way up the line post. It fooled me so many times into thinking it was locked up, it was a cunning bird and did it to my brother and sisters when they dared enter our backyard.

Even our friends were targets, in the end none of them would go into our backyard not even when told the chicken was locked up. If any child ventured into the backyard they always ended up the line post. Rita Hill, who lived across the road from us, remembers being terrorised by our chicken. She said she was up the line post shouting, "Pross! Pross! The chicken is biting me!" She hated that chicken as much as I did and so did my sisters.

I shook the gate one afternoon after school, waiting to get attacked when I noticed Lonesome was hanging over the drain, blood dripping from it. I thought at that time, this is the happiest day of my life. As I walked into the living room my mom was crying her eyes out. "What's wrong Mom?" I asked. "My chicken is dead," she said. I'm not sorry, I thought, I hated it. My sister Kathleen told me later, when we were talking about that chicken and having a laugh, the reason Mom had its neck screwed was because it was egg-bound and suffering. When it was on my plate I sank my teeth into it, I felt like I was getting my own back. The girls, however, wouldn't eat it.

If you walked into our backyard as a child, this is where you would most likely end up, shouting, "Mrs Prosser! The chicken is pecking me!"

34. NAILED

Whenever Trevor and me went to our park, we sometimes took a shortcut down passages between the houses, much to the annoyance of the residents as they were for their use only or access for the dust men. At the end of the passages was a 6-foot fence and some children had broken a couple of the palings off to gain access to the park, as the park entrance was at least a couple of hundred yards away. We used those passages whenever we went to the tip or to play in the park, it saved us a good walk.

This particular day we went to the tip, I suppose we were there about three hours, looking for pram wheels and bicycle parts. On our way back to go up the passage we found someone had nailed a big board where the palings were missing. "Gosh," I said, "we now have to walk all that way to the rotten entrance." (Rotten was a word I used all the time). I kicked the board in temper, as I did it swung, "Ay, Trev," I said, "look at this." I was pushing it with my right foot and for some unknown reason enjoying it, what I didn't notice was the nail coming out from the fence. When it did finally come out the nail went straight through my kneecap and stuck out the back of my knee. The weight of the board knocked me to the ground, for a few seconds I was panicking, as I sat wondering what to do. Trevor was even more panicky than me. Who can I get to help me I was thinking, no one is around. Trevor was shouting and dancing around in uncontrollable fear. I looked around for help but still not a soul was anywhere to be seen so I took hold of the board and as quick as I was able, I pushed the board up and out came the nail. Boy, that was some pain, I can tell you. I rubbed my knee and limped home. You know I never washed that wound or put anything on it, it was very sore the next morning. It healed up all on its own, it never went septic. I never told my mom, I don't think she could have taken much more of my antics. That knee is giving me a lot of trouble now, it gives way every now and again, I'm not sure if it is because of that nail or just old age.

35. TRAIN JOURNEY

One year I went with the school to Weston-super-Mare, it was a day trip and my first holiday by the sea. We saved 3d a week all year until we had paid (£1), most times I ran errands to pay my 3d for that trip as my mom could never afford it. Well, now and again she would give me 2d, but in the main I ran errands to help pay for myself. Of course as a child sometimes, well most times, I would spend my money on going swimming or going to the pictures (cinema that is) with my mate Trev. But on this occasion I was paid up, my mom gave me a one-shilling piece, that's all I had to spend. My clothes were washed and ironed even though washing and ironing worn-out clothes didn't help them look good or much better, well a little maybe, but at least they were clean and smelt nice. No children commented on my clothes, they were used to seeing me like that and they were all too excited to even bother I'm glad to say.

So, we all gathered at the school, I only lived a few yards away. Most of the parents were there to wave their little son or daughter off. I used to think how sissy it was to have your mom wave you off, dads were at work. In those days, looking back, I would have loved my mom to wave me off. We walked in file from Audley Road School, Glebe Farm to Stechford Station, I loved that station it was all wood and the wooden steps down to the platform were wonderful.

I've loved station buildings and trains all my life. A lot of moms were also at the station to wave off their little ones. I looked to see if my mom was there but I knew she wouldn't be because as I left home, she was doing the house work. Oh well, I was so excited anyway, a train journey was better than the seaside to me and my mind was on the fish and chips we were going to have at dinner time. We were all talking very loudly, full of energy, I remember they were all telling each other how much money they had to spend. Not one of them had less than a pound, one had £5. I was thinking, how can their moms afford that? I suppose I was thinking they were all as poor as we were in my family, but what a lot of money for a child in those days. Yes, I was jealous, of course I was. I've thought about this a lot. Green with envy is perhaps a better way to describe how I felt.

When we got to Weston it was a wonderful sunny day and the station at Weston, I loved it and still do. We walked again in lines of two to the beach, one exciting moment for me was to see and smell the sea, it looked to me like a giant of a seafront never ending.

What I've thought about all these past years is, all day long I was walking around Weston-super-Mare, on my own. I had no one to talk to, was it because I only had one shilling or was it that I didn't have enough money to go on the fair with them or was it that they were so excited they just took off and couldn't wait to spend their money? As far as I know they were in twos or groups. I've never known why I was alone, it could be other reasons. I went looking for a present for my mom with my shilling, I was walking round all the shops but no way was I able to find anything. I kept an eye on the time as we were told to meet by the pier at 12 noon.

We all met up where we were told to on the sea front and the teachers walked us to our dinnertime restaurant upstairs to what I thought was a palace, the waitress came out with a beautiful plate of fish and chips. I was starving. It was a wonderful dinner then a nice cup of tea. Out we all went again and were told where we should all meet up at four o'clock, so in the afternoon I walked around again on my own again looking for a present for my mom with a shilling, I was hoping, wasn't I? I looked in a shop where they were selling ice creams, I bought one for 6d. I thought with the 6d left I could buy my mom a present, whatever could I get for 6d for a present? There wasn't anything for a shilling, how or why I thought I could get her a present for 6d I've no idea. I started to feel quite guilty and ashamed, I had bought an ice cream but a 1/- or 6d would not have got a present for my mom. Almost time to go and meet on the seafront, I had looked really hard for a present and no way could I get one, so I bought another ice cream with my 6d. I felt really sad I couldn't buy Mom anything, all day all that was on my mind was buying my mom a present, then the guilt really kicked in when my shilling had gone.

We all met up at four o'clock and started the march back in lines of two to the station. When we arrived at the station, I was looking at all the iron work, the shiny bricks and the wood work on the station platform, it looked beautiful to me. I was in heaven, I do still love that side of life. On the train going back it wasn't quite as noisy as the train in the morning, but still noisy; the noise ceased quite a lot I think after about half an hour. Then it went sort of quiet and they started to say what they had bought for their moms and dads. Some had bought statues, postcards, sticks of rock even novelties. I went nearer the window looking out of it, hoping no one would talk to me.

They did of course, I don't know, as all daylong on my own not a soul to talk to now they wanted to talk to me and I didn't want them to. A girl with red hair, I've forgotten her name, said, "What did you buy for your mom and dad?" I pressed my face up against the window pretending I was looking at something and making believe I couldn't hear her. The boy sitting next to me was pushing me saying, "She is talking to you," pointing at the girl opposite me. I'm sure I had a red face, I had to turn and talk to her, again she asked, "What did you buy for your parents?"

"Nothing," I said, I only had a shilling.

"He hasn't bought his mom and dad a present. You are horrible and mean. Did you hear that he spent all his money on himself and hasn't bought his mom and dad anything? You are selfish." Girls are so cruel at times, I felt terrible. I could have done without her comments I was feeling bad about not getting Mom a present as it was. "Well I've bought my mom and dad a present," she then put her tongue out at me and turned her back on me. To hide my embarrassment, I pushed my face up against the window, by this time I felt really ashamed of myself, so for ages I just watched the telephone wires going up and down as the train flew past them (it still fascinates me to this very day) by this time no one was talking to me.

Suddenly I noticed we were approaching Stechford Station, there was pushing and shoving to look out of the window to see if they could see their moms. When the train stopped, they all went for the door at the same time. I stood out of the way and let them all get off the train as I knew my mom would not be there. There were moms and dads by the dozens it seemed. I stood out of the way. When I got onto the platform, as it was very crowded, I heard such wonderful things said to the children by their parents, "Hello darling", "Hi sweetheart", "I've missed you", "Oh it's good to see you", "Did you enjoy yourself?" Hugs and kisses, they even brought coats for their little ones. I waited to see if my mom was there, I knew she wouldn't be. All was quiet, I was standing on the platform on my own, I must confess a little tearful and I felt very lonely at that moment. I waited till they had all gone. I looked around to see if Mom was there, I was standing on that platform and there was not a soul to be seen. I walked up those wooden stairs, it was now so quiet I could hear myself breathing, as I reached the top of the stairs I was still hoping my mom would be there. Not a soul to be seen. Oh well, I thought, so I walked home.

I got to my house, not a soul was in sight. Boy, I felt so unwanted (I was wanted, of course, my mom loved me) but for a child to go through a day with all those people everywhere and no one to talk to is, to say the least, soul destroying. So I went round the corner to the British Legion which was just at the back of my house, I walked in (the doorman knew me) and my family were there. Just to end the day, worse than I thought possible, my mom held out her hand for a present. She must have thought I was trying to hand her something, I bowed my head in shame saying I couldn't buy her a present. I think that moment was the lowest point of my young life.

That was the first time I went with the school to Weston-super-Mare. I went to Weston a couple of years after that, but once again I had only 2/- to spend and that was given to me by the headmaster Mr Taylor. At least I had a day at the seaside, which I was very grateful for, as I'm sure many children didn't have the opportunity to go.

36. OUR DUCK LONESOME

Again, just like before, we had another twelve chicks that were kept in the cupboard next to the cast iron fire grate. Where they were purchased from, I again have no idea, my eldest brother Donald always got them. Any road up, one by one they died off, just as they did before, that used to sadden me. A few weeks later there was only one left, the difference being this one turned out to be a duck and it wanted to be the boss. A pen was built in the backyard in the same place where that fiercesome chicken, Lonesome, had its pen.

This duck wasn't fierce, it did just what it wanted to do and again the only person that could control the duck just like that chicken was my mother. Whatever she told it to do, it did. A little reluctantly sometimes but she always made sure it obeyed her. Just the same as we had to obey her, my mom took no nonsense from anyone. When she said do it, we did it, when she folded her arms and gave what I can only describe as a stern look, we knew she meant it and so did her duck.

Now who would have thought you could train a duck? It just proves that animals have brains and like us must be thinking. One day, so my mother told me and this happened a few times, she was walking up the road to the shops when she noticed people were laughing at her. Not being very well off and her clothes looking a little worse for wear, she was thinking that something must be wrong with her coat or (as she put it) her dress was tucked in her drawers. People would smile and say, "Hello, Mrs Prosser," for everyone in those days knew my mom. When she turned round to check her clothes were in order, there walking behind her was her duck following her up the road.

Mom told this story many times over the years that's how I remember it so well. She would point her finger down the road saying, "Go home." The duck would turn its head and look at Mom who would say, "I won't tell you again, now get home." That rings a lot of bells in my memory of my mom saying those very words to me over the years. As the duck looked back at Mom it looked like it was saying, "Please let me come with you." Just like me and my sisters used to say to her, we got the same response that the duck got from her. Off the duck went straight back home, it never wandered, it went straight into its pen. It's a wonder it was never attacked by any dogs because in those days dogs used to roam around free.

When I got home from school one evening just like that chicken, Lonesome the duck was hanging over the drain with blood dripping from it. As I walked into the living room, Mom was sitting at the table crying her eyes out. Mom was very soft like that even with us when we hurt ourselves, she was very strict when it came to good manners. When I asked her what was wrong, she replied, "My lovely duck has gone." She cried the same when the chicken had been killed. It is wrong to give any animal a name when you are going to eat it but that duck was really one of the family.

37. CIGARETTE CARDS

Jimmy was a boy me and my friends usually never played games with. He was very good at making paper aeroplanes, one evening he made one and he threw it, it went round and round and round in circles, it was fantastic. I tried many times to fly paper planes, every time I tried to fly my plane it just nose-dived straight down.

Anyway, Jimmy had a biscuit tin full of cigarette cards that his granddad had given him, or it may have been his dad. He would sell us some cards, about twelve cards for 3d (three pence), but he insisted we played him at skimmers so he had the chance to win them back. He always won them back. What we did would be to stand one card up in the gutter and from the middle of the road we had to skim a cigarette card at the card standing up in the gutter and try to knock it down. The one who knocked it down won all the cards that had been missed.

We could be standing in the middle of that road for hours, well it seemed a long time, we didn't have a problem with any vehicles. Thinking back we were very lucky children we could play in the horse road all day long, playing all sorts of games with no traffic to interrupt us at all. The children these days will never experience the happiness of playing in the street day after day like we did, I loved those days.

I never ever beat Jimmy at the game of skimmers and to my knowledge no one else ever did. Every time he knocked the card down, he would shout, "Jen!" this was his favourite saying. We must have ruined some rare cards but of course they were worth next to nothing in those days.

38. BEING A ROUNDSBOY

At the top of my road a man named Arthur used to deliver bread door to door, he was a little wiry man with curly black hair and he always wore a brown overall known as a cow gown. He worked for a bakery company called Harding's Steam Bakers, their factory was based in the area known as the Swan in Yardley. At that time they had horses as well as petrol vans, I used to love seeing the horses being groomed and cleaned out. I even went to the boss (who wore a white coat, that's what most of the bosses wore then) and I asked if I could help with the horses. "You are too young, son," was his reply, "you aren't allowed by the horses at your age." I couldn't believe it. Sometimes when the men brought out the horses from the stables, they would ask me to hold onto the reins for a short time which made me feel all grown-up.

Arthur drove a petrol van and one day when I was walking home from the shops he was getting out of his van, I asked him, "Can I help you deliver your bread?" "Okay," he said, "I leave the depot at 7.30am." "Okay, I'll be there," I answered. Great, I was thinking, I can earn some money, but no wages had been mentioned. I was there by 6.30am, the face of the bus conductor when I asked for a 3d child's fare! It was just gone 6.00am when I got on the bus and for a nine-year-old he must have thought I was just too young to be out at that time in the morning. I walked into the bakery and was stopped by a man wearing a white coat, "What can we do for you, young man?"

"I'm working with Arthur," I said.

"Oh, you mean Mo," the boss said. Funny, I thought, why does he keep calling him Mo when his name is Arthur? It was a few days later I asked one of the roundsmen tending the horses, "Why do you call Arthur, Mo?" With a laugh he replied, "If at any time we call across the yard to him, he always shouts back 'half a mo'." "Oh," I said, not really understanding.

It's strange to think now, that then they allowed children around places like that at such a tender age. Being fascinated by the horses, time would fly by and I would get distracted by them. Mo said in a stern voice, "I've been waiting for you, if you don't buck your ideas up, I won't let you help me again." I ran to the van and he lectured me all the way to the start of his round, saying I had made him late and I would have to run when delivering the bread to make up the time. We delivered bread to Northfield, the Lickey Hills and surrounding areas, we always stopped at the pub or should I say public house or boozer, as my dad would refer to them. Every dinner time, it seemed like an eternity waiting in the van, he was always over an hour in there. He never gave me a second thought or worried if I had any food or a drink, he was a different person when he left the pub, I couldn't talk to him as I could before he went in there.

When he had finished and completed his round, he would pick a man up who worked on a building site, this man was also a neighbour and only lived a few doors away from my house. I had to sit in the back of the van, squeezed up against the bread trays which were made of wire and the back doors – that was the most uncomfortable ride I ever experienced. I was bounced about like a tennis ball.

I only suffered it for three weeks then I didn't go again. He only paid me 1/- (a one shilling piece), it had cost me 1/3d (one shilling and three pence) in bus fares to travel there, so I used to walk home and the walk must have been five to eight miles. I'd had nothing to eat or drink, well to be honest I used to pinch the corners off the uncut loaves and hide a packet of morning coffee biscuits and eat them when he went into the pub and dispose of the wrapper down a drain in the road. I asked customers if I could use their toilet just so I could have a drink of water from their tap. Why did I stick it out for three weeks? The promise of more money next time, but that never happened.

Milk rounds, I thought I would try, so I asked the milkman if I could help him. He delivered all around the streets where I lived and it was in the six weeks school holidays so I could work all the week. He said yes and he paid me 1/- (one shilling) for the week. Trouble was I'm a true Brummie (really, I suppose you could refer to me as common) and I talked using a lot of slang words, he was always telling me off for saying "bo-ul" instead of bottle, "nunk" for nothing, "goo" for going and "belly" for tummy. I got so afraid to speak I would just nod my head when he said anything to me, even that made him have a go at me, "Lost your tongue now have we?" I just couldn't win with him and when I told him I couldn't read the notes in the empty milk bottles I got another lecture, he told me his little boy was only five and could read and I should be ashamed of myself, "Don't your parents help you?" He went on and on at me all day every day, "I will have you speaking the Queen's English in a few weeks," he told me. You wunt, I thought to myself, when you pay me I wunt help yo agen. "Ask your mom to wash your clothes and you have a bath when you get home," he said to me.

I was a bag of nerves, I only stuck it for a week and I did that just to get my shilling wages from him. On the Monday I was sitting on my front gate when I heard him shout to me, "Come on! I'm not waiting all day for you." I jumped off the gate, shouting as I ran down my path, "I ain't helping yo agen." So that was that.

I sat on the gate again after he had gone. As I sat there, I spotted the Corona pop man, so I ran over to him, "Can I help you, Mister?" "Okay son, but mind I won't stand any messing about."

"Okay Mister, I wunt," I replied. Their bottles in those days had a white porcelain stopper with a red rubber seal and the stopper was held down by a heavy-duty wire that when pulled downwards tight to the neck of the bottle would seal the gas in and stopped the pop from spilling out. I enjoyed working for him, the first Saturday he gave me a bottle of pop and 2/- (two shillings) after that he gave me 1/- (a one shilling piece) plus the bottle of pop. I could only work with him on a Saturday because he delivered in other areas during the week. He insisted that when I helped him on the next Saturday, I must return the bottle as there was a two pence deposit on it. He was very kind to me and he said he liked me because I wasn't cheeky and I worked hard.

One time I asked if my friend Trevor could help him as well. "Okay," he said, "but I will only pay you 9d (nine pence) each and you can share a bottle of pop." Great, I thought, me and Trevor we always worked well together. I know I got a little less money but Trevor was still my closest friend, we shared what we had anyway. We helped the Corona pop man for a very long time, then one Saturday he told us we weren't allowed on the lorry anymore, one of the other roundsmen had a boy working with him who had fallen off the back of the lorry and badly hurt himself so all the roundsmen were told they could no longer have young children working for them.

One day a lorry was going slowly down Trevor's road and a young lad was running backwards and forwards to the lorry, he was leaving paper bags for old clothes to be put into them. I was stood talking to a boy named Barry who went to my school and he said let's ask the man

Corona bottles.

in the lorry if we can help. He said, "Okay lads, I will pay you half a crown (2/6), and I'll be back in two days' time to pick all the bags up." We worked hard all day delivering those bags to every house in the area and he came back two days later, we met him at the top of Trevor's road. We picked up all the bags filled with clothes and threw them into the back of the lorry, at the end of the day he only paid us 1/- each (a shilling) instead of half a crown. It seemed that children were always taken advantage of by adults, we had worked very hard for our money.

39. PAST DREAMS

I've been told lots of times that I shouldn't live in the past but I can't help it. Poor as I was, knowing hunger, cold, living in well-worn clothes, doing hard work and running around in the snow until I could no longer stand with frozen fingers and soaking wet feet, I still loved my childhood for the sunny days, playing and earning money.

Cycling I really enjoyed and the warm days with my friends. I now sit in the garden on a sunny day, feet up, close my eyes and remember my childhood days with my friends. On cold winter nights with lights out and a glow from the fire (now of course it's a gas fire), feet up, all is quiet, nice and warm, my mind's eye goes all through my childhood days that's how and why I remember so much. Things like my friend Trevor and his sister when they used to come swimming with me and my sister Janet. We all ran errands to earn money for swimming. We even went scrumping apples together, not for devilment, that was food to us. We did have our childish moments, like climbing over the railings into our school playground, climbing up the drainpipe and onto the roof. All the roofs were flat and every time the caretaker, with his two sons and an Alsatian dog, would catch us and throw us out. Mind you, thinking about it, he was very good, he never once told the headmaster, we would have got the cane for sure.

Swancote Road, where Trevor lived, was a long road with eighty or ninety houses maybe more. One night, being a bit bored, four of us went to the top of the road and then ran, jumped, dived or rolled all the way to the bottom of the road over the gardens. We never trod or broke any plants down – mind you, most people didn't have flowers in their gardens then just lawns. Other times we would tie cotton to door knockers, pulling the cotton to knock the door and running away, most children did this I would think. Rolling little mud balls and throwing them at the windows, even grit if we had no mud. Yes, I was a normal child in that respect. I didn't annoy the neighbours very often. My friends and me would just play and enjoy life.

I lived in a corner house so from my back garden I could see a lot of back gardens in the next road, four back gardens from mine was a very big apple tree, it grew the biggest cooking apples I have ever seen. One memory that is very vivid is that one night me and Trevor climbed over the hedges of the back gardens to this apple tree. We got two apples, they must have been six inches across, sour but we were hungry so we suffered them. Well, I could only eat half of this apple and Trevor only managed about the same but we never wasted any of the apples we saved the half we couldn't eat till the next morning. Next day we were walking down the road and the man whose apple tree it was, called us over and shaking his finger at us said, "Don't you ever steal apples from my garden again." I've no idea how he knew. "If you want an apple you knock at my door and ask for one." I'm not sure how many days went by, three or four, and Trevor said, "Go on Dave, ask him."

"No you ask him."

"No you ask him." So I knocked on his door and said, "You said if we wanted an apple to knock on your door and ask for one." Well, he looked at me and Trevor and in total amazement and disbelief, he replied, "You cheeky little buggers," (lots of adults used that word then) "wait there." He came back with a big apple and said, "Half each and don't ask again." Shaking his head as he closed the door, saying again to himself, "cheeky little buggers."

There are so many memories that come back when you sit quietly, close your eyes and start to think of your childhood. The good parts and the bad parts, the freedom I had as a child gave me much happiness.

40. THE RUBBISH TIP

As a young lad of six, I spent many hours on a rubbish tip behind the Atlas Cinema, as I've already mentioned I was looking for shoes for my mom to burn on the fire. Also, I was looking for old bicycles parts as I was hoping to make up a bike. One of the times I got a tyre off a bent-up wheel, a few weeks later I would find a good wheel, a pedal, then a chain and a frame – it took months. One day I finally found a saddle with no covering on it, I was so pleased I wrapped rag all round it so it could be sat on with some comfort.

As a small boy I would ride my sister Kathleen's bike but I couldn't sit on the saddle and reach the pedals, it had no brakes and it was a girl's bike so it had no cross bar. I could stand on the pedals and with my arms up straight I could hold the handlebars. Down the hill I would go, I realise now it was very dangerous of course, but as a youngster I knew no fear. Anyway, there weren't many cars about in those days, mostly horse-drawn carts, so down the hill with no brakes was quite safe car wise. I used to jump off when I got to the bottom of the hill, I ruined the clothes I had on, mind you they were worn out anyway, made worse with me enjoying my life as a youngster. Poor Mom, she used to darn and repair my clothes on an almost daily basis.

I had the surprise of my life one day when going on that tip, finding an old bike, all rotten and bent up but with brakes on it back and front. Well, I carried it back to a friend's house whose dad very kindly got the brakes off and saved one of the cables, I was so pleased (what wonderful people in those days, always ready to help). It was a very long time before the back brake was fitted but I had that bike for many years. Tyres, I always found them on the tip, worn but still okay well almost okay. I even found a wheel one day, a back wheel complete with tyre and cog, in the river with air still in the inner tube. I did change the girl's frame to a man's frame, a girl from school gave it to me, it had been left at the back of her shed, it was rusty but okay.

Trying to become a road user.

We call those times the good old days. I was very poor, with shabby clothes but funnily enough I was very happy when away from school and playing with my friends. But I always wanted better at the time. I was ridiculed, pushed around by teachers, had the mick taken out of me and was tormented because I was scruffy. But now, I sit and think about those days with much fondness and wonder was it so bad? Would I have liked to be better off, warm, well-fed and have a nice bike? You bet your life I would. I did get a better saddle – yes, off the tip.

41. TEA UNDER THE APPLE TREE

Pype Hayes Park is a park near Erdington. My mom took me there once with my little brother John, he was in arms, only a baby. We went with my mom's friend Winnie and her son John, my friend, we were there all day. Our moms took sandwiches, bottles of water and a bottle of pop, no sweets or cake just sandwiches. We had a great day, me and my friend John. All there was in the park was a river, well a river to me was the nicest playground any child could ever want. I never went there again, only the once, but the memories I have of that day will live with me forever.

The other place my mom took me to was a place called Sutton Park, we went there twice, none of my mates were with me, it was just my mom, my two sisters and my younger brother. What a big park, I remember walking for what seemed miles. There was a fair there and the twice I went with Mom there was a train running all round the outside of the fair. I had a ride on the train the first time I went. The second time my mom said, "Don't ask me for anything because I have no money." There is a stream there and I played in the stream all the time we were there. Whenever I went anywhere there was always a river to play in. I wonder do children do that sort of thing now?

Another place my mom took me to was a place called Chelmsley Wood, there wasn't a river but there were lots of trees to climb, bushes to hide in, millions of bluebells to pick and lots of rhododendrons it was a magic place to visit. One memory that will never fade about Chelmsley Wood was that is the first and only time I went with my mom on my own it was just Mom and me, where the rest of the family were, I have no idea. We got on the bus at Glebe Farm, went through Kitts Green, then Lea Village and got off the bus at Tile Cross, walked towards Marston Green Village past a pub called The Bell and up a road to the edge of Chelmsley Wood.

We walked along the edge of a field and on the right was what was known then as the mental hospital, next to Marston Green Maternity Hospital. We walked along the path at the end of it and straight in front of us was a farmhouse, in its grounds was an apple tree. My mom told me to sit under the apple tree while she went to the house. She came back and sat down beside me, the sun was shining, it was a wonderful

My mom took me to Chelmsley Wood to the farmer's house shown in this picture. The grounds were open then with no wall not even a road just a dirt track path made by the farmer's farm equipment, it was mostly a wood. In the grounds there was an apple tree just about where those conifers are, sadly it's been chopped down. We sat under the apple tree and the farmer's wife came out with a jug of tea, not a pot a jug, and two cups no saucers. Wonderful memories.

warm day, no one was about then what I suppose was the farmer's wife came out with two cups and a jug of tea. That's stands out in my memory, sitting under the apple tree with my mom and a jug of tea. I was very happy, that's why I remember that day so well.

Many a year later I tried to buy that farmhouse and would you believe it, I ended up living in that road where that house is, it's known as Berwicks Lane now, they built hundreds of houses on the woods and that apple tree was still there then. I told my family every time we passed the house that I sat under that apple tree with my mom and had a jug of tea. The council bought the house and cut the apple tree down and built a wall all around that old farmhouse. I felt they had taken a little bit of me away.

42. TIDDLY WINKS

Coronation Day 1953, a magical time. I was very excited, tables were laid all down the road with more food than I ever remember seeing before, so much sweet stuff. Everyone was laughing and smiling it was a very happy place to be. I lived in Plowden Road, Glebe Farm in Stechford (as I have mentioned before) and they had laid the tables for

Coronation Day, 2nd June 1953, author's family from left to right.
Back row: Kathleen, Dad, Doreen, Mom. Bottom row: Janet as the
Queen of Hearts, John as Little Red Riding Hood, me as a clown.
My two sisters Kathleen and Doreen made the costumes for the
fancy-dress parade out of crepe paper.

Coronation Day group photograph of neighbours and friends from Plowden Road, Glebe Farm, in the playground at Audley Road School.

Plowden Road at the top of the hill. I was sitting at a table in Swancote Road, Trevor's Road, all my friends came from Swancote Road. I really should have been in my road but I wasn't, I have never known why, Trevor's mom squeezed me in. I would love to see a photograph of Plowden Road and Swancote Road with all the tables in the road, someone must have a photo of them.

My friends all had a dicky bow tie that lit up but I had nothing, I was jealous, I felt left out. I was wondering why everyone else had something but I and my sisters and younger brother had nothing, present wise that is. I made a pig of myself with the food. Then we went to my school for the games, all my family were there. We were all dressed up for the fancy dress competition, my eldest sisters Kathleen and Doreen made our costumes out of crepe paper. My younger sister was the Queen of Hearts, I was a clown (I was always told I was a clown by my mom, that's the reason I was dressed up as a clown), my youngest brother was dressed up as Little Red Riding Hood, you can see us in the photograph.

We didn't win the fancy dress competition. When it came to the games I entered for the running because I was fast, I thought if I win, please don't give me Tiddly Winks, I hate that game (I still do). I was hoping for a gun or a car, but no, what did I win? You've guessed it a box of Tiddly Winks. My sister and little brother played with the game but not me.

When we were playing games at my school we all grouped together for a photograph. I still have photos of that day with me dressed in crepe paper as a clown and I'm glad I am able to share them with you in this book.

We had a big bonfire in the middle of the road for the Coronation, I remember going around all the houses in my road to get any item they were throwing away for the bonfire. I collected all sorts of things 78 RPM records, sideboards, chairs, trees, old timber, even toys. I went to one house where the man said, "Hang on a minute, I'll look in my shed." What a shock when he came out with a rocking horse. He saw the look on my face, he then said, "No, I will put it on the bonfire myself, if I give it you, you will take it home and give it to your little brother." That's exactly what I was thinking and he knew it. My little brother would have loved it. I was very disappointed.

The bonfire was really good on the night and when they lit the fire there was so much furniture burning, I wonder how many would-be antiques were burned that day all over England.

There were fireworks, it was a wonderful time, potatoes were roasted in the hot embers. While I was standing there watching it all I noticed the rocking horse burning, what a shame, my brother could have had so much fun on that horse. Mind you he had my rocking horse to play on.

Wonderful times and wonderful memories.

43. THE CORN SHOP

In our house we were disciplined by our mom, she ruled with a rod of iron, never our dad. Mom was the driving force. Off our kitchen was the coalhouse and that's where Mom kept the cane, knowing it was there in the corner of the kitchen made me think twice before doing anything wrong. I still got out of line sometimes and then Mom would say, "coalhouse."

"Sorry, Mom," I would say.

"If I have to ask you again you will get double three whacks across the backside," it kept me in check. I needed that discipline because I was a little rogue. I always knew when my mom was angry, she folded her arms in an austere way and I knew that was it. After I was caned, I had to put the cane back in the coalhouse. When I walked back in, she would kiss me on the forehead and say, "Now be a good boy."

One day I had the bright idea that if I broke up the cane, she would not be able to use it, so while Mom was out at the shops I broke it up and put it in the dustbin. The next day while playing in the road with Trevor, my mom called me into the house and asked me to go to the corn shop, "Here is three pence, go and buy me a nice thin cane, one with a nice thin end."

The corn shop was called Turners and they sold corn, fertilisers, pigeon food and sacks of oats. I used to buy oats from there for our family to eat for breakfast and there used to be mice droppings in them! A scoop was used to measure the oats into a brown paper bag, this scoop was also used for all the animal food, but the person serving did not know they were being eaten by my family and probably other families in the same position as ourselves.

So I went to the corn shop and I looked for the thinnest cane I could being very particular about the one I chose, I shook the cane to make sure it had a really good whooshing sound. I gave the money to the man wearing his brown cow gown that I had always seen him wear as far back as I could remember.

Walking back down the road I thought, my mom will love this, talk about being thick! Into the house I went, "Here you are, Mom. I picked the best one," and with that Mother bent me over and really gave me six of the best. Hurting, crying and very bewildered I asked her what she had hit me for and told her I had been a good boy. She said, "You broke the cane up and put it in the dustbin and thought I wouldn't see it didn't you, now you can put this cane in the coalhouse." So, Mom made me go to bed and I went with a backside ringing and stinging. If only I had covered the cane up, I was saying to myself when I put it in the dustbin, maybe I could have saved all that pain? I would love to be able to say I never got the cane again but that wasn't the case I got it more times than you can shake a cane at me, I never learn, I think if they could cane me now it would be almost on a daily basis.

44. MAKING SLIDES

One very cold winter's evening I went out playing in the horse road, it was covered in deep snow. All my friends were out playing, it was so cold I nearly went back into the house, in fact it was well below freezing. One of the boys said 'let's make a slide' so we all got buckets of water and poured it in the middle of my road as it was quite a steep hill. We started the slide just outside my house and it ran to the bottom of my road, across Swancote Road that ran across the bottom of my road over the pavement and to the garden hedge of our friend Rita Hill. The slide must have been a hundred yards long. We left it to freeze all night and the next morning I started to slide down the hill across the road, at the bottom the snow was so deep I catapulted over the hedge into Rita's garden. That evening all my friends were out sliding and we were very happy kids.

With all the sliding, the ice became like glass and when the baker came down the hill with his horse and cart, the horse started to slide down the hill. I was so worried for that horse I cried, thinking it was going to hurt itself (I'm a big softy). The cart went sideways and pulled the horse away from the icy slide, the deep snow in the road brought the cart to a halt, I was so relieved and from that day to this it made me respect horses. My mom asked me to run up the road to the shops, she always said run. I was cold and wet standing by the fire, I just didn't want to move so I said, "Mom, I'm cold." I didn't want to go to the shops. So she put her coat on and said, "Oh, I'll go myself, it'll be quicker." As she walked across the road, she stepped onto our slide, Mom fell over and hurt herself quite badly. I felt very guilty and with tears in my eyes I said, "I will go to the shop." She was laid up for about two weeks after that fall and whenever she asked me to run up the road after that I did. Ash was put on the slide, well it was a danger to horses and people, but it was fun while it lasted.

The snow in the garden must have been 5ft deep, maybe even more. I remember the hedge next door to Rita's garden was very high and the snow in that garden was even deeper. Me, being the smallest and skinniest kid of them all, I was constantly being thrown over the hedge. I landed in the snow and got buried, I disappeared under the snow and I found that to be very frightening at first. All the lads had a very good laugh at my expense, made worse for me when the girls came out to play and the lads were showing off in front of girls. I went over the hedge quite a few more times. I was by this time very wet, shivering, frozen and feeling very uncomfortable. The girls were very well wrapped up in wellingtons, hats, scarves and gloves. The boys never wore scarves like the girls did. Me, I was in short trousers, shirt, coat, socks with more holes than material (I used to tuck them under my feet, which meant they couldn't be pulled up) and of course pumps with holes in, no gloves. I was enjoying life, playing with my friends. Trevor was dressed the same as I was, as he was as poor as me. The lads, of course still showing off around the girls, pulled off my pumps and my worn-out socks held them up in the air and shouted, "Hey, girls, do you want a pair of socks like these!" That was very embarrassing to see the girls laughing at me.

That same winter Trevor and me made good money by shovelling snow from paths. I never liked shovelling snow and still don't. There were six of us lads all together, but it was only ever me and Trevor that tried to earn money as they all got pocket money but Trevor and me didn't until we were much older. This was because my dad was a very heavy drinker and didn't like parting with his money. All the pubs that my dad drank in have now been demolished, I often wonder if it's because my dad stopped drinking there!

WHITE WINTER

It Was Winter And I Was Small,
No Underwear Had I, No None At All,
The Clothes I Had Were In Poor Shape,
I Played In The Snow And Thought This Is Great,
Not For Long For I Got Cold,
I Was Only A Child And Not Very Old,
All My School Days Were Like This,
Children Loved To Take The Mick,
No Wellies All My Young Life,
Holes In My Pumps, Well That's Life,
Pumps In The Snow Well We Were Poor,
That Was My Life, That's For Sure.

45. LAND OF THE SPITFIRE

Castle Bromwich Aerodrome used to have open days, how often I'm not sure. At the front of the aerodrome on a stand used to be a Spitfire and I loved going there as a young lad, I was captivated. I always went there with Trevor's brother Tony, I never remember Trevor going. Seeing all the air men in uniform made me think, I'm going to be in the air force when I grow up.

The one thing that has stuck in my mind was a long glass case with an aeroplane attached to a length of wire that stretched from one end of the show case to the other with hedges, building and a bell on the bottom in the middle of the scenery. The object of the exercise was to release the bomb from underneath the plane by pressing a button when the plane came along. When the button was pressed the bomb would fall and you had to hit the bell. After a few goes, I hit the bell every time. The RAF man said, "You are too good now," and stopped me using it. It was great fun.

I watched the paratroopers jumping out of a barrage balloon, I loved to see those big parachutes open, they are bigger than they look when they are on the ground. My wife's uncle was a paratrooper, I must have watched him jump out of that balloon many times.

On the next open day I couldn't wait to have a go on the display model again. I went in and said to all the boys there, "I can hit the bell every time." When my turn came, I said, "Watch this, I never miss." Well, I couldn't get near the bell, not once did I hit it. Serves me right for being so big headed, that day taught me a good lesson to keep quiet and not brag.

46. SNOW HILL STATION

Trains are one of the loves of my life. There were two stations I really loved, both were in Birmingham – one I've so many fond memories of one was Snow Hill and the other was Stechford Station. Both stations are still in use but, alas, were knocked down and rebuilt, nowhere near as good as they were before. The old timber and stone work to me was majestic.

One wonderful memory I have of Snow Hill Station is a green stamping machine with a big brass arrow in the centre of it and the alphabet all-round the outside. When I turned the arrow to each letter in turn and pulled a big lever on the side of the machine it stamped out the letter that had been selected. Me and Trevor printed our name out on that machine every time we went to that wonderful station, it only cost a penny a go and it came out stamped on a strip of aluminium. We were thrown out of that station more times than I care to remember by one of the porters, for no other reason than we were kids. Never playing up, we always said the same thing, "We have a platform ticket, mister." They always said the same thing to us, "I don't care, out you go," that was the normal reply.

I was in heaven with the smell of the locos I can smell it now, if only they could bottle it, all train enthusiasts like myself would buy a gallon of it. I adored seeing the trains coming and going, it was a thrill for me to see the motion of the wheels and the valve gear all moving together, to be honest I still get a kick out of it. The day they started to knock Snow Hill Station down I had a tear in my eye, I can tell you. It was a massive loss to the people of Birmingham, we lost a beautiful masterpiece and I just cannot bring myself to go and look at that modern rebuild. I will live on my memories and the original station will live in my mind's eye forever.

47. IN AWE

Every time me and Trevor went into town we liked to walk around the market, one of my favourite places was Nelson's Column by St Martin's church, watching the escape artists trying to escape from the chains they were bound in. The blind lady always fascinated me shouting "handy carriers", she was there for years, I was privileged to buy a carrier from that lady for my mom a time or two, God bless her.

If we had any money, we always made a beeline for the man selling baked potatoes for 6d a spud, he used those white cone-shaped paper bags, same as the ones they used in sweet shops when you bought 2oz of sweets. He put salt in the bottom of the bag and the spud on the top, we loved buying those spuds in the winter time, it was great to stand next to the oven and feel the heat from it on a cold Saturday morning. One Saturday we went to see him he said, "Hello, boys, nice to see you again do you want a potato?" "We only have 3d each," I said. I was expecting him to shout, I'd had my share of being shouted at I can tell you, but Trevor and me were never cheeky. "Okay, boys, a small one for 3d." They weren't that small they seemed as large as they normally were, I think that potato seller was being kind which Trevor and me didn't experience that often.

48. FAITHFUL FRIENDS

Our dog Rex was what my mom would call a Heinz varieties, he was a cross between a Jack Russell and anyone's guess. He was white all over except for a brown patch on the middle of his back, we went everywhere together, we were pups together. Rex was a very loyal dog.

One day me and my friends were walking to Saltley when they decided we should catch the bus, we got on the bus and I forgot my dog Rex was with us. Tony said, "You forgot your dog!" I felt really bad that I had forgotten him, boy did he run fast after that bus. I was calling him, "Come on Rex, come on boy," he jumped on the platform of the bus and I was so relieved. I took him upstairs, all my friends made a fuss of him, he loved it, he licked their faces until they looked clean. Where we were going, I'm not sure, where we went that day I have no recollection of it at all. I remember that part of the day I've just written about because I felt so bad about Rex, leaving him when I caught the bus.

A long time after that I was with Trevor and we were just walking around the shops where we grew up, in the evening we usually walked around the shops or sat on the wall of the Glebe pub. A boy came up to us that I knew by sight because he went to our school, he lived a few yards away from the pub. He asked us, "What are you doing round here?" "Nothing," we replied. "Clear off," he said, "this is my area, not yours." "I will go where I like, you can't stop me," I replied then he went to punch me. Rex, from a standstill, flew at the boy and grabbed his arm, well I was so surprised I never knew my dog would protect me like that. I was so proud of him, the boy backed away from us, whimpering with fear. "Come here Rex, good dog," I said, making a fuss of him.

The boy ran away shouting, "I will fetch my big brother to you." I proudly shouted back, "Yeah, I will set my dog on him." I was so shocked my dog had saved me from being beaten up. About five minutes later I

Those bullies were not as tough as they thought
they were when confronted with my dog Rex.

saw the boy with his big brother, they were the bullies of the area, as they were coming towards us his brother looked really angry, I was scared stiff I can tell you. "Is that them with that dog?" I heard him say. "Yes," the younger boy said. He walked up to me and he went to punch me, Rex flew at him, well I could not believe how scared of my dog he was. As Rex went for him, he half turned in fear. Well I saw something you only see in cartoons because Rex missed his arm and caught the back of his trousers, the boy was spinning round in circles with Rex outstretched going round and round. This big boy was whimpering louder than his little brother had, who was now running down the road so fast he nearly fell over. Rex gave up his grip and came running to me. The big boy was so scared, as he was running away, he was shouting, "I will get the police, they will have your dog put down." Brave boys soon became cowards when faced with a growling dog.

I never heard any more about that incident, it never happened again but it made me love that dog even more. Rex lived with us for many years, the only food he ate was what we left on our plates and we fed him biscuits, cake, not often as those two items we only had on rare occasions, and bits of chocolate at Easter. In fact no matter what it was, Rex would eat it, no fancy tinned dog food in our house, if there had been I think for sure we would have eaten it ourselves.

One evening when school was finished for the day, I walked into the kitchen of my house when I heard a loud sobbing noise in the living room. Mom was sitting at the table sobbing her heart out. "What's the matter?" I asked. Rex was dead, I was told. We had one car a week or fortnight down our road and it seems Rex saw a cat and ran across the road straight under a car, this is what the man told my mom. He very kindly carried Rex and put him in our back garden, I dug a hole in the front garden and buried him. It's a shame I haven't one photograph of Rex, our faithful dog, but he gave me many happy memories.

49. BUTTERFLIES

At the back of my house, a few gardens away, was a piece of waste ground and in it there was a big hole in the ground, I used to catch newts there. I was told by one of the boys that had a motorbike, who used the hole as a scrambling circuit, that the hole was made by a bomb. He would ride his motorbike in and around that hole, I was always worried he would hurt the newts. I think it was a natural hole made by Mother Nature herself, mind you it had all sorts of rubbish in it. Would you believe bedsteads, old prams with no wheels and of course garden rubbish – how those newts survived in there is a mystery to me. Years later the hole was filled in and they built a British Legion on the ground, since then that building has been demolished, now lots of houses stand there.

Before all those changes took place when it was a big hole with newts breeding in it, I also caught butterflies there. I was chasing a beautiful coloured butterfly with a net made from one of my mom's old stockings tied to the end of a twig, the stocking kept coming off so I held the stocking at the end of the stick so it wouldn't come off anymore. I caught two butterflies then I spotted a Bob Howler as we called them, I ran to try to net it, tripped and badly cut my left wrist right down to the bone. Off to the hospital again, this time it was four stitches.

I did make my mom's life hard. Sorry Mom!

50. FLYING HIGH

Model aircraft were not a great love of mine, I liked them okay, but at that time I never wished to own one. Trains were the love of my life. After running errands one week I did really well, so I went to town to a model shop in Temple Row, opposite St Philip's cathedral in Birmingham city centre. I loved that model shop, there were aeroplanes hanging from the ceiling and other made-up kits, it truly was an Aladdin's cave, I used to go in to just to look around. I purchased a Tiger Moth aircraft kit, it was all in balsa wood, I can't remember the cost of it. I hurried home with visions of flying it in a few days. Allow me to explain the reason why I bought a balsa wood aeroplane kit.

What persuaded me was, as I was walking up the road to our shops with Trevor one morning, a boy we knew but never played with came out of his entry carrying a model aeroplane. It was beautifully painted and Trevor said, "Corr, Bobby, can we have a look at your aeroplane?" We walked over to him and asked him what the plane was called. "A Hurricane," he told us, he had only finished it that morning. "You can look at it but no touching," he had put an engine in it and he flicked the propeller with his finger to it started. What a row it made for a tiny engine! We walked down the park with him and he started the engine off. Corr, I thought, I want one of those. Then Bobby said, "If you are really interested, I will show you how to put them together and dope them." Dope was a word used at Trevor and me, I only knew the word because that was what I was called all the time, I had no idea it was a term used for making aircraft outer skin hard. So we went back to his house and waited for him in his back garden and out he came with all manner of items. He got some tissue paper, pasted the dope on it, "That's what you do, then you place it over the frame of the aircraft." He said, "It goes taut when it dries like this," and showed us an unpainted one. It's really amazing how taut it goes.

Did I say flying in a few days? Well, it looked easy when Bobby was showing me. When I got my own aeroplane kit home I was trying to study the plans but not being very bright I just could not work it out. A couple of days later, I must try, I thought to myself so I laid out the plans and tried

The flying game, never to be. Attempting to make a balsa wood bi-plane.

to glue all the struts together for one of the wings. I glued them to the plans, I broke some struts, some got twisted and that was the end of that plane. I only got as far as putting a wing together badly. I wished my dad would guide me but no such luck. A few months later I did buy another one but I made the same mistakes again, that kit never got past one wing, it too ended up in the dustbin. What I needed was an adult's guiding hand but it never happened. The trouble as well was I didn't have any craft tools, I only had my mom's carving knife. Talk about doing everything with nothing, but I couldn't have done it even if I had everything.

51. BACK GARDEN ADVENTURE

Billy lived in Swancote Road with his granddad, mom, dad and sister. He was better off than all the rest of us put together, he had a tandem bike, a touring bike trolley, a tent, games, good clothes and binoculars. He was a wiry little fellow. One day he said to me, "I've got my tent up in the back garden, come down tonight you can sleep in it." It was the old green thick canvas type. Off I went at eleven o'clock that night. I told my mom, "I'm sleeping at Billy's tonight." She didn't mind, she just said, "You behave yourself."

I waited eagerly for Billy to open his back garden gate. How he got out of his house without his mom or dad knowing was he climbed out of his bedroom window, slid down the drainpipe and let me in the backyard. Being in the summer it wasn't total darkness and Billy had a torch with him to guide us right across the yard where there were two sheds with a flat roof joining both sheds making a passageway to the back garden where Billy had his tent. I slept in that tent all night, it was quite an adventure.

The next morning after his mom and dad went to work, Billy came to see how I had liked my stay. "Great," I said. "Good," said Billy, "any time you want to do it again just let me know." I never did stay there again, when I told the other lads they all said they had done that a few times. Great memories of doing those sorts of things.

As I walked through the passageway one day, Billy opened the shed to get his bike out and there in all its glory was the oldest motorbike I had ever seen at that time. It was in beautiful condition. I asked, "What's in the other shed?" When he opened the door, it was like Aladdin's cave – tools hanging up, what a wonderful workshop. No wonder then, whoever it was made Billy's trolley made a fantastic job. He also had stilts. I always wished at that time I could have all those things. But whatever I got, I adored it and loved it. Billy loved all of his possessions but I don't think he had quite the feelings I got when I acquired anything, when things are not easy acquired. I don't think it's possible to have the same feelings as earning and working hard for them, I may be wrong.

That motorbike I saw in Billy's shed ended up in the motorbike museum at Bickenhill.

52. SCHOOL HOLIDAYS

One day in the six weeks school holidays I went to the tip, I could not believe my eyes, there in all its glory was the bottom half of a pushchair. It had all four wheels and was in good condition, being a pushchair and not a pram the wheels were the small type and not the big ones that a pram has. I was so excited to see those wheels they were like finding gold. Wheels were never thrown away in the 1940s, people always made use of wheels in those days and never ever threw them on a rubbish tip. They were always used to make carts for fetching coal and taking rubbish to the tip.

Any road up, I picked up the frame with the wheels still attached and ran all the way home, the reason I didn't try taking the wheels off at the tip was I was afraid some bully boy would take them off me. Oh yes, there were those types around even in those days, I had my share of being bullied by older boys, I was a tough little fellow and strong but I was a placid boy, I hated arguing and fighting so I did neither, I liked the peaceful life.

When I reached home, I set to and started to clean the wheels. I love things to be clean, after saying that, can you imagine the state I was in? Oh yes, in a state alright but at that moment in time I didn't care, I was the king of our street, I had four wheels plus the axles. Right, I thought, now all I need is a plank and two pieces of wood to fit on top of the axles, so I kept going back to the tip. It was about six weeks before I found a plank it was five feet long, one inch thick and ten inches wide if my memory serves me right. After finding the plank I needed lots of nails, so back to the tip I went several more times to find the nails I required. I found half a house brick which I used to get the nails out of the wood I found that with my hands pushing the nails back and forwards I eventually got the nails out, it took me days to get the number of nails I needed, but I did get extra ones just in case I needed them.

With a pocket full of rusty nails, I walked home, the nails were in my trouser pocket which was the only place I could carry them, every step I took I was injected in the leg a dozen times. I suffered that because the nails were so important to me as I hadn't a coat at that time so it had to be the trouser pocket (did you know a boy with half a house brick and a piece of wood can demolish a house!).

I straightened all the nails in my backyard with the half a house brick, well I hadn't got a hammer. I nailed the two pieces of wood to the axles, I then nailed the axle to the back of the plank and the front. Boy, was I proud. I was now the owner of a trolley, I was so pleased with myself. Ah string, I suddenly thought, yeah my mom's washing line, there was lots of spare rope wrapped round the line post because it was too long, so I went and found Mom's scissors and helped myself to a long length of it (I got a good hiding for cutting the washing line). I lit the gas stove put Mom's poker in the flames until it got red hot then burned a hole at both ends of the piece of the wood attached to the front wheels (I only used the poker to burn the holes in the wood when my mom was out shopping). Then I tied the rope through the holes I had made, just the job I thought, then I pulled my trolley up to the shops.

The first shop was called Stockton's, it was our local newsagent and outside the shop was a good slope so I pulled my trolley right to the front door, sat on it and away I went. This is great, I thought, down the slope I've got to turn the front wheels, they won't turn! What do I do now? So, I pulled hard on the rope to turn left and pushed the right-hand side of the front wheels with my right foot, as I did the front axle came off. I went flying and grazed my knee, as I sat on the pavement rubbing my leg a man walked past and asked me what had happened. "My front wheels have come off," I explained. "What you need, son, is a nut and bolt, if you make a hole through the plank and the axle, put in the bolt then you will be able to turn the front wheels." "Thank you, mister," I said. What a nice man, I thought, he didn't laugh at me or ridicule me like everyone else does. What a fool I am, I said to myself, of course I need a nut and bolt.

I carried my trolley home, got my mom's poker from the fireplace, lit the gas stove and put the poker into the flames till it glowed red hot like I did before (again I could only do it when Mom was out). I saw my dad make holes this way there were no tools in our house, I then burned a hole in the plank. This took three goes before I got a hole through the plank and a further three times to get a hole through the wood on the axle. I knew my mom was short of money so I put three pennies in the gas meter, it was money I had earned from running errands, she never knew I did it and couldn't understand how she got so much gas for her one penny.

When my dad came home from work, I asked him if he could get me a nut and bolt from work where it was easy for him to get nuts and bolts. When I showed him what I wanted it for he was so proud of me, "Did you do this all on your own?"

"Yes," I replied. With a pat on the head he said, "Well done, son." I felt very proud, he had never praised me up before (or since). "I will get your nut and bolt tomorrow," he said.

The next evening I kept pestering my mom, asking is it time for Dad to get home yet? I must have asked a dozen or more times till in the end she just ignored me. Well, I was excited and very impatient, I just wanted to get my trolley on the road. When he finally walked in I said, "Have you got it, Dad? Have you got it?" "Gad blimey," his favourite saying when he was annoyed, "let me get my coat off." He handed me the nut and bolt with washers and he explained how I should fit it.

I fitted the nut and bolt just the way Dad had showed me. Up to the shops I went, outside the newsagent's shop doorway I sat on the trolley, down I rolled, pulled on the rope to turn left, round I went. It felt great, I was really excited. Trevor saw me, "Corr, Dave," he said, "whose is the trolley?"

"Mine, Trev," I answered, "I made it all from the tip when you weren't with me. I thought I would surprise you."

"Let me have a go, Dave?" Trevor asked.

"Okay, Trev, don't crash it." He loved it, I got quite a big head, I had never done anything myself before.

The next afternoon all my friends had a go on it and my other friend Billy said, "My dad has made me one, I'll go and get it."

"We can have a race," I said to him.

Billy laughed at me and said, "What yo race me on that old wreck?"

"Yeah, come on, Billy," they all shouted, "Okay, okay, I'll go and get it."

Well, when I saw his trolley my heart sank, I can tell you, it was painted green and red with a padded seat and white lining all round it, I thought it was beautiful. All my mates were laughing at me by this time, "Well you threw out the challenge," said Eddy.

Racing Billy downhill on my trolley that I had made up from the tip.

119

"It's okay," I said, "You never know I might beat him." Well, that gave them another good laugh, I was dying inside with shame as we both sat on our trolleys. Billy sat high on his trolley, he had big pram wheels on the back and small ones on the front, I only had small wheels all round on mine – his small wheels were bigger than mine. As we sat on our trolleys a young girl walked past, Billy said, "Ay love, he has challenged me to a race who do you think will win?" I felt my face go red, "Oh yours will easily," she said. "See, Dave," he said, "I told you."

I said, "Okay, Bill, a rolling start no pushing."

Off we went and to my surprise and delight I was much faster than Billy downhill, he only passed me when we hit the flat level road. "That was a fluke," Billy said to me, so we did it three more times and I beat him downhill every time. I shouted, "I'm the king of the hill!" Boy, did I feel proud. He had a beautifully made trolley that his dad or granddad had made for him, mine was made up from scrap off the tip that had cost me nothing. That taught me a good lesson that day, never to judge a book by its cover, as the saying goes. I had years of fun on that trolley, do you know for the life of me I cannot remember what happened to it.

53. THE RIVER BLYTHE

Coleshill is a little village in North Warwickshire, the first time I ever went there was with my next-door neighbour Barry, as I've already mentioned. My mom took me there once on the bus, then a couple of years later I went to the same spot with my mates on a bike I had made up from the rubbish tip. It seemed like there were hundreds of people walking up and down Maxstoke Lane to the same spot. It was a field with a river running through it, known as the Blythe, and was at the bottom of a steep hill. People were having picnics there, children were paddling and me and my mates went there to swim.

There was a little white cottage known as Cuttle Cottage, the field was Cuttle meadow and the little bridge over the river was Cuttle Bridge. Opposite the cottage was a wooden shed that had been turned into a tea hut, that's all there was and a lot of the time the tea hut wasn't even open. One hot day we were getting a cup of tea from the hut when Billy went to the dustbin at the side of the hut, he picked up a stone and started to kill the bees that were buzzing round the bin, when he suddenly jumped up screaming a bee had stung him on the lip. Boy, within seconds his face had swollen up like a balloon and his lip went three times the size it normally was!

I never took a towel to dry myself with I just used to run around till I got dry. One very hot afternoon a man came up to me and asked if I would sell him my swimming trunks, "No," I told him.

"I will give you half a crown (2/6d)," he said. I was tempted.

"All right, five bob (5/-)," he said.

I answered with, "They won't fit you."

"Yes, they will," he replied, "they tie at the sides, okay 7/6 (seven shillings and six pence)." That was a fortune to me.

"Okay," I said, so with Johnnie's towel wrapped round me I took off my trunks. He gave me the 7/6d and without a care he undressed without covering himself, to say they fitted where they touched is an understatement! But he was happy and so was I.

I was telling Robert, who lived next door, about the field in Coleshill. "I want to go," he said.

"Your dad won't let you," I said.

A day at Coleshill. We swam in the Blythe a lot almost every summer.

"I won't tell him, Dave, I will take my tent if you let me go with you."

"Okay," I said. So, without his dad seeing, he passed his tent over the fence to me and I tied it onto the back of my bike, it was thick green canvas with wooden poles, to a young lad it felt very heavy.

Next morning I met Robert round the corner, he sat on the crossbar of my bike off we went. It was a struggle, we kept changing over so we had a break from the pedalling, but we got there. Robert loved it and it was a pleasantly warm day. Then to my surprise my mom turned up with Johnnie's mom. It started to rain so my mom and Johnnie's mom went into Robert's tent, poor Robert stood outside getting wet, he wasn't very happy. Mind you we were dripping wet from swimming in the river. The rain stopped, the sun came out and we had a great time again.

I took Robert a couple of more times after that but without the tent. As I was swimming against the current, Billy who always played up, picked up a dried cow pat and threw it quite hard, it hit me just below the shoulder blades and took all the wind out of me, plus it felt like a thousand injections. I was fighting to stop going under and I swallowed a fair amount of water, I nearly gave up when I felt the bottom of the riverbed, the water only came up to my backside as I stood up. I thought it was much deeper, as I stood up emptying my lungs of water, shouting to Billy, "Yo are mad Bill! I thought I was going to drown." Billy was on the bank laughing his head off. We never fell out. Billy always did silly things like that, but we all were great friends, we looked after each other. We had a fantastic childhood.

My mom always said, "These days are the best days of your life, young man. Enjoy them, son, as much as you can." So I did, thank you Mom. How right she was.

54. GAS WORKS

Trevor came to me one day, he said, "Dave, Mrs Dovy wants a quarter hundred weight of coal." So we went to Whites coal yard in Church Lane, Stechford. In all weathers we would carry coal – wind, snow, rain, frost – nothing stopped me and Trevor from earning money. We got 3d sometimes 6d (sixpence), in snow we always got 6d. Mrs Dovy gave us a shilling (1/-), that was a lot of money to us.

We never had a wheel barrow, I used to carry the coal while Trevor held it at the back. I asked him recently if he did ever hold it to help take the weight off my back, he said, "No I didn't." No wonder my muscles got bigger! I am 66 now, Trevor is 67 and we often reminisce about our young days and the things we did to make a penny.

When I was carrying the coal, I carried it till it got too heavy for me then I used to drop it, have a rest for ten minutes then ask a man that was passing to put it on my back. I got comments like "it will kill you," or "it will break your back." After it was lifted on to my back, I would again carry it until I dropped it. We would do this until we carried it to where it had to be.

I feel at this point I must mention that neither Trevor nor me had any wellies, gloves, overcoat or underwear on whenever we did any errands, we even had pumps on that were worn out. The reason we always had worn out foot wear was because it was the only footwear we had, and when worn daily they would be worn out in a couple of weeks. Our clothes came from jumble sales and were always too small.

I remember one day it was snowing and very slippy underfoot. Mrs Rowly asked us if we would fetch a quarter hundred weight of coal, this we did many times for her and usually we were paid 6d (sixpence) as we were carrying the coal back to her house. There wasn't many men about so it took much longer than normal to get it to the house. The deal was we would get a 1/- (one shilling) that day for fetching the coal because of the bad weather. Any road up, when we did finally get back to the house, cold, wet and worn out the lady said, "Where on earth have you been? I've been waiting for this coal to light the fire for when my husband gets home from work. You have been messing about haven't you?" No explanation would do, she just wouldn't believe a word I said. "It's the snow, Mrs Rowly, it's slippy and there weren't any men around to lift it onto my back and there was a long queue." "You're lying to me, well I'm only giving you 2d each," she replied. Two pence, we were always polite, "Thank you, lady," I said. Whenever she asked me or Trevor to run errands for her after that we said, "No." But we said it very politely.

We were used by a lot of adults who didn't care about our welfare, we worked hard for them but they never appreciated what we did for them. One or two would say, "You are good lads for fetching these groceries for me, I can't pay you anything today, I will see you all right next time," but they never did, and we were too polite to remind them. Mrs Rowly asked me and Trevor if we would go to the Gas Works to get a quarter of a hundred weight of coke, of course we said "Yes" even though we had said we would never run any more errands for her. So she gave us a 1/- (one shilling) that was for the bus fares (3d each way) and said she would give us sixpence for getting the coke. I can't remember how much the coke was, I said to Trevor, "If we walk there and ride back, we can save the bus fares." Halfway there it started to rain so we had to get on the bus after all because it was taking far too long to walk.

On arrival at the Gas Works there was a very long queue, so like everyone else we had to stand in line. The rain was very heavy and by this time we were soaked through to the skin. We paid at the office, got to where the coke came down a shoot and the man operating the shoot asked if I had another sack, "No, mister, I've only got this one it's okay."

"Shame," he said, "I would have filled another one for you half price."

"I wouldn't be able to carry it," I explained.

His tone changed then, "Go on get out, there are other people waiting. Bloody kids," he said to the next customer, "you wouldn't think parents would let kids out on days like this." As we struggled to get the sack on my back, I heard him say to a man, "Have you got another sack?" So he asked everyone, he made his wages up that way I suppose.

I carried the sack of coke across the road to the bus stop, by this time the rain had soaked the coke through the sack, which made a black slurry run down my back. As we waited at the bus stop the rain now was really heavy and coke or coal wasn't allowed on buses. When the bus arrived the conductor was upstairs so we got the coke onto the luggage rack, fortunately there were no pushchairs on there – and away we went. After a few minutes I looked round to make sure the bag of coke was still there, to my horror there was black slurry running from the sack off the luggage rack along the platform and off the bus. The conductor was going mad, "Who owns this bag of coal?" he was shouting as he ran up and down the stairs, "I will find out whose it is." The conductor hadn't noticed how wet and dirty we were.

"Don't look round, don't say anything, Trev."

"Okay, Dave."

"When we get near our stop Trev, if the conductor goes upstairs, I'm jumping off."

"We will have to carry it then, Dave."

"I don't care, Trev, I'm jumping off, you stay on if you want to." "No, I'm with you, Dave," replied Trevor.

The stop before ours a lady got off the bus, fortunately for us the conductor ran up the stairs still shouting, "Whose is this bag of coal?" This gave us the opportunity to jump off the bus without him seeing us, but as we stood up, I noticed how wet and dirty the seat was. I was very worried thinking someone else would sit on that seat and ruin their clothes. As the bus started to move, I said, "Now, Trev," and with every ounce of strength left in me I grabbed the sack, threw it off the bus and jumped after it. The conductor was fuming, "I will remember you, look

TAKING HOME
THE COAL

A. WAITE

*Going to the Gas Works to get a bag of coke, getting very dirty and
soaking wet, then to be told you are not getting paid makes
it a day neither Trevor nor myself will ever forget.*

at the mess you have made on my bus." It was still raining hard, I got on
my knees and picked up the coke that had fallen out of the sack, I got
hold of the sack, got it on my back and with Trevor's help I stood up. The
black slurry from the coke was running down my back and my legs into
my pumps, I was as black as the coke inside the sack, we were soaking,
dripping wet. Now my feet were very sore from the gritty black slurry

running into my pumps. When we got to the back door of the house Mrs Rowly opened the door, she was very angry, "You've been far too long, you've walked to save the bus fares haven't you?"

"No, Mrs," I said.

"Look at the state of you, your mom won't half give it to you when you get home, you are black and soaking wet."

"It's the rain, Mrs."

"Don't be cheeky to me, young man." I never meant it the way she took it.

"Well, I'm not paying you, here is a biscuit each." It was a Rich Tea biscuit, stale and soft. She always gave us a biscuit and they were always stale. Upon that she closed the door.

"Look Trev, we are soaking wet, black and four hours' work for a rotten Rich Tea rotten soft stale biscuit."

"Why does this keep happening to us, Dave?"

"Dunno, Trev, it's not fair all that work and no money."

To cap it all I got a good hiding off my mom. Bless her, she had to repair my clothes. Well, it wasn't the last time we worked and never got paid.

55. TRYING TO MAKE BOTH ENDS MEET

One of the things about Christmas that I loved, as well as getting presents on Christmas Day, was going into town with my mom and seeing all those lights, every shop was decorated up. There were always long queues inside and outside Lewis's. I only queued there once with my mom to see Father Christmas at Lewis's, it took a long time to get in and all those people on those concrete stairs, to be honest it used to scare me. I always worried about stairs like that sticking out of the wall, nothing underneath them and just sitting on the floor either end of the stairs. Going through the grotto was magical for children but I much preferred the Co-op Christmas grotto, it always seemed bigger and better to me. All those wonderful toys and me, like all children, wanted them all.

I went up town with Mom every year at Christmas but most times she had no money to spare. We always went round the Rag Market and the Meat Market, Mom was looking for cheap presents for her children and cheap meat. I can still see and hear in my mind's eye dealers holding toys up with outstretched arms shouting, "Only one left 6d, take this toy with this one then you can have the two for 9d – they are here to be sold." I used to think, I wish I had some money I would buy those. The man I loved to watch was Mr Lees, he was the man selling the china with an overturned tea chest and a piece of carpet on top of it. He would bang the plates on it and throw them up in the air and say, "These plates will last you a lifetime and they are strong," all the time banging them edgeways on, by hitting them on the tea chest this way they wouldn't break. Christmas is a magical time.

One year I was in town with Mom at Christmas, she was really poor that year, she desperately tried to buy toys cheap. I can see her eyes now looking so anxious and watery asking, "Can you do those for 3d or 4d?"

But no good, the dealers wouldn't drop the price. She was so worried, the pain she must have been going through just trying to get little presents for her children so we could wake up Christmas morning with something in our pillow case, yes always a pillow case. That year I remember seeing tears run down my mom's face and I asked, "Are you alright, Mom?" She said, "I've got something in my eye." I knew she was hurting, it's hurting me writing it down. I had 8d in my pocket and offered it to my mom. "It's alright, son, buy yourself some sweets," she said. I went to a stall and saw a very pretty glass decorated with holly and bells, it was 6d so I bought it for my mom. "Here you are, Mom, I've bought you a present." She broke down and sobbed her heart out, with her arm round me she hugged me very tightly, she never said a word at that moment in time but her actions said it all. How can a child not remember such an occasion? As we walked out of the market she did say, "I love the glass you bought for me, but I can't buy you anything." "I don't want anything, Mom," I replied. I hurt her more than I could ever have imagined by trying to make her happy with a present, I shouldn't have done it, but as a child who loved his mom so much, I thought a present would make her feel good.

When we got to the bus stop to head home there was a very long queue, it seemed never ending. We waited for over an hour to get on the bus and it was filled to capacity with people standing from the front of the bus right down to the platform. I hated being squashed and pushed around on those over-crowded buses. As it approached the next bus stop there was a very long queue because the bus had filled up from the terminus, it didn't stop and the people standing there shouted and waved their fists. I was so relieved to get off that bus. Every year was the same, too many people, not enough buses in those days at Christmas time, a day in town meant a day.

56. RATION COUPONS

Stocktons, our local newsagent, was on the corner of Trevor's road, Swancote Road and Mr Stockton ran that shop all through the war and well into the post-war years. One Sunday I was sent to the shop to buy a pound of sugar, it was against the law to sell groceries on a Sunday in those days. My mom said to me, "Son, I've run out of sugar. Go to Stocktons and get me a pound of sugar."

"Aw, Mom they wunt serve me it's Sunday."

"Well you won't get any pudding then," she replied. Well the thought of pudding changed my mind.

When I asked for a pound of sugar a silence came over the shop. The lady looked around to see if any policemen were about, she very quietly walked to the backend of the shop and still looking around she picked up a pound bag of sugar. It was a blue bag, I think all sugar in those days was put in those blue bags when the shop keeper weighed it up themselves, covering the bag with both her hands and placing it under my coat. She said in quite a worried voice, "There, keep it under your coat and don't let anyone see you with it." I was terrified, I put it under my jumper and I ran like the wind down the road non-stop till I got inside my house, I felt like a criminal. It was a relief to walk into my house, my heart was going like a train. "Here you are, Mom, sugar, I'm not going on a Sunday again," I said. "Okay, son," she said very calmly like nothing mattered. I'm standing there shaking. To think these days I could walk all around Birmingham with a wheel barrow full of sugar on any Sunday and not a soul would even take a second glance. How our England has changed.

The nicest memory I have of that shop was the day rationing finished. I was sitting in the house when I was told I could go and buy some sweets without ration coupons, my mom gave me 3d (three pennies) and I ran to Stocktons and very nervously asked for 2oz of sherbet lemons. I have no idea why I remember what sweets I bought, maybe because I was scared to death waiting for the lady to ask for sweet coupons or because it was the first time I had ever bought sweets on my own because all I had ever known was everything with sugar in it was on ration coupons. With shaking hands I handed over my 3d, the lady handed me the sweets and said, "There you are, bab." I got out of that shop very quickly in case I was asked for coupons.

I will go and tell Trevor, I thought, it will excite him. "Trev, Trev," I blurted out, "you can buy sweets without coupons."

"I know, I've been already with my mom, she bought me some," Trevor said. I was so disappointed, I thought I was the only one that knew, but it appeared all my friends knew before I did. Well, at least I had my 2oz of sherbet lemons.

One morning, when rationing was still in force, I was going through the sideboard draws looking for some string. My sister Doreen had shown me how to make a gate when the string was tied into a circle and put on each hand, then with the fingers put in certain positions and pulled apart, the string took on the shape of a gate. I pulled out what I thought was the drawer but I pulled out the middle piece between the two drawers by mistake, to find it was a secret drawer I never knew was there. In it I found Mom's ration book so I cut two sweet coupons out, they were the last two sweet coupons, then I ran up the road to find my mom. "Mom, Mom!" I said, "I've found these," and handed the coupons over. "Shh," she said, "don't let anyone hear." She took me into the sweet shop and bought me 2oz of sweets, dolly mixtures if I remember. I thought I had been very clever, I thought she will never know (children know nothing, do they?), I had taken her last two coupons.

The next day I was playing with Trevor in the horse road, "David!" Mom shouted, "I want you a minute."

"Oh Mom, I'm playing," I said.

"Just for a minute," Mom said. As I walked through the front gate, she grabbed my arm and said, "You little bugger, you took those coupons out of my book that you gave me yesterday."

"I found them, Mom," I said.

"Oh, you still want to lie to me, get the cane from the coal house," she angrily replied. She caned me three times for stealing the coupons and another three for lying to her. I never lied to her again (well little white ones). No tea that evening, it was five o'clock in the afternoon, I was in bed with a very sore bottom. I very much needed that sort of discipline, if my mom had been soft with me I dread to think how I would have turned out. Spare the rod and spoil the child, how true is that saying.

57. RUN RABBIT RUN

Christmas carol singing night after night, I never got to that magic £1 mark, close with eighteen shillings and eleven pennies, but never the one pound. A couple of my mates did. It's a magical time for children with Christmas carols, coloured lights, Christmas trees and all the trimmings – how I loved those magical Christmases. Coming from a family with not a lot of money it was make-do-and-mend season, a magical time for me but not so for my mother, the suffering she went through I can only imagine.

My mate Johnny came down the road one Christmas Eve, he told me, "Your old lady is up the shops crying her eyes out." He heard her say to a lady who wondered if she was alright, "I've got no money to buy my children any presents for Christmas," her heart and soul must have been torn in two. Just writing about it makes me feel tearful, that memory never fades. I actually remember what I got that Christmas, a colouring book with a cowboy on the front and with about eight pages in it, six crayons, no nuts or chocolate and no orange, we usually had those at Christmas but not that Christmas. I kept that book for a very long time I've no idea why, maybe because I felt there was so much hurt in my mom or maybe I kept it to say thank you, maybe I thought it was my fault. I loved it and it was very special to me, the pictures in it were of Hopalong Cassidy (William Boyd).

There were happy times, like making paper chains, I remember the horrible taste after licking the gum to stick them together and crepe paper cut into strips and twisted, then pinned to the ceiling. Sometimes my sisters would sew cotton right through the middle of the crepe paper strips, then they would gather it up to make it looked fancy instead of flat twisted paper.

There is one year I remember so well, but not what year it was, I was very young. It's strange how certain things in your life stay as vivid memories like it was only yesterday. It was Christmas morning, well 12 o'clock dinnertime, and I was lying on the floor in the living room as it was the warmest place in our house. I had a shooting game that Christmas for my present, it was a little wire gun which, when I squeezed the handle, released a spring that fired a round piece of wood at four animals on a frame. When hitting one of the animals, you scored points which were shown on the front of the game underneath each of the animals. My mother was putting the dinner out and shaking potatoes from the saucepan onto the plates on the table in the living room, there was lots of steam and Mom said, "You will have to move now, son and play with that after dinner." Flanagan and Allen were singing *Run Rabbit Run* on the wireless (no TV in our house in those days), I loved that song and still do. That very special Christmas morning is burned into my memory and will be mine to eternity, I love it. Thank you, Mr Flanagan and Allen.

One Christmas in 1948, when I was five years old, I had a cowboy suit and it meant the world to me. On the first Friday at school after Christmas we were told we could bring a toy to school, "I will come in my cowboy outfit," I said to the boys. Another boy said he would come in his too, I heard him telling another boy about his outfit, boy did it sound good. My mom saved 3d a week in a club to get my outfit. Any road up, I didn't go in it to school, to be honest after hearing about the cowboy outfit the other boy had I knew they would laugh at me and take the mick because my outfit was a cheap one mostly plastic or a material like plastic. I was glad I didn't because his outfit had sheepskin leggings, a waistcoat, a cowboy shirt, the hat had stones that looked like diamonds all-round, guns with pearl handles, gun holsters with diamonds on them and diamond-studded cowboy boots with silver spurs attached – it was the best outfit I've ever seen, even to this day. Mine was very basic but it was mine and I loved it, I made-believe I had forgotten it and you can imagine the comments I received, "I bet you haven't got one", "bet yo dain't get any presents for Christmas" children are so cruel.

That same Christmas morning my sister Doreen had a doll, as she went to walk down the stairs she tripped and dropped it, the doll

Playing with my shooting game on Christmas Day, listening to Flanagan and Allen singing Run Rabbit Run. I loved it, and still do, it made that Christmas morning stand out in my memory.

smashed into a thousand pieces, did she sob. We only got one main present but some years we got a game as well. Every Christmas, Trevor and me went Carol singing, with the money I got I bought my mom a tin tray and a pinny from a shop called Lathams. The lady never asked me what size did I want and when Mom put it on I remember saying, "Oh, Mom, it's too small." She always said, "It's perfect, I love it." Bless her, buying for my mom always made me feel good and very happy.

AUDLEY ROAD SECONDARY MODERN SCHOOL
Showing the infants' playground where I played on my first day at school.
The wooden building was divided into two classrooms: on the right was the
infants at that time in 1948, on the left was the juniors. I was taught in both
classrooms. That building has since been demolished.

AUDLEY ROAD SECONDARY SCHOOL
This is the juniors' playground. The wooden buildings in the background
are classrooms. The window facing was the Headmaster, Mr Taylor's,
office. The brick building on the right was an air raid shelter and next to
that was a wooden building that was the boys' and girls' toilets.

137

AUDLEY ROAD SECONDARY MODERN SCHOOL
The low brick buildings shown were air raid shelters built in the Second World War. Entrances were bricked up and they too have now been demolished. Me and my friends used to climb in them after school. They were at the far end of the junior school playground. The grass is where we practised our football sometimes, but most times it was on the concrete playground. I played centre forward for the Juniors Football Team. Happy days!

58. JUGS OF BEER

The Glebe Pub was my dad's second home (more like his first) and any spare money or minutes he had was spent in there. That pub was the major reason why me and all my family suffered the poverty that we did. The Glebe has now been demolished and my mom, bless her, would have raised the Union Jack if she had seen it being demolished.

It had an outdoor and lots of children, including me, would earn money for fetching beer from this outdoor. I've taken beer bottles, jugs, pop bottles, once even a basin, usually for a pint of mild. They weren't supposed to serve beer to children but they always did. I was given 3d (three pennies) by one lady and 4d (four pennies) by another, never the men, only ever the ladies used to ask me to fetch beer.

Sometimes the men serving would be very grumpy and say in a raised voice, "Don't keep coming here for beer, I've enough to do." I used to think, why say don't come here for beer because that's what they sold? In the main, the barmaids were nice, only a couple of times I remember them saying, "I'm busy, you will have to wait," and wait we did for what seemed to be forever. Most times they would say, "I'm not supposed to sell you beer," but they always did.

59. PIG SWILL

A friend of mine whose name was Douglas (or Dougie as I called him) lived at the bottom of the adjoining road to my road, his dad kept pigs in their back garden, they did this all through the war because of food shortage. I loved to watch the pigs being fed, when the food was being poured into the trough the pigs went wild, like they had never been fed, they pushed each other violently. It fascinated me so much I offered to go around the houses with Dougie and collect the pigswill, it was a smelly job but I just loved doing it.

Dougie lived across the road from Billy, two doors away from John, Eddy lived across the road from John, Trevor lived six doors away from Eddy and I lived over the road from Trevor. The six of us spent many a year going everywhere together then as we entered our teens we sort of split in half, but not completely because we sometimes all got together and went cycling, swimming or playing football. Me and Trevor were like brothers, we spent every day together and Johnny sort of mixed with all of us, out with them one day and us another.

About once a fortnight Trevor and me would help Dougie collect the pig swill which was in dustbins usually at the side of the houses. We could only go to certain houses because there was another family that kept pigs a few doors away from Trevor's house, they never touched Dougie's pig bins and he never touched their pig bins. As we were collecting the swill one day, Dougie looked really worried, "What's the matter, Dougie?" I asked. "There isn't enough swill for the pigs," he said. His bin round was done in two halves, one set of houses one fortnight and the other half the following fortnight. In those days people didn't waste much food, well it wasn't long after the Second World War and rationing was still on, and times were still very hard for the working classes so pig keeping was even more difficult. "Well, Dougie, let's take one or two and half empty them from the other pig keeper's bins." I said to him. "We can't, Dave, we have an agreement we don't touch theirs and they don't touch ours."

"Well, what if we don't empty the bins and only take a bit out of each bin Doug?"

"That should be all right, Dave," so that's what we did. When we got back to his house he said, "I haven't any firewood to boil the swill up," so I climbed over the fence to the field at the back of his garden to find some wood. Dougie said, "I've looked all over that field, Dave, there isn't any." Wood was very hard to find in those days, everyone used wood to light their coal fires, I looked and found a small handful in the field. So with the few sticks I found and with what Dougie had, he lit the fire under the pig swill.

As the wood started to burn Dougie began to throw the bread on to keep the fire going, "I hate burning the bread, Dave, but it's the only way I can get the swill to boil." I never knew bread would burn like it did (okay I know I'm thick but we only find out things as we go through life). All sorts went into that swill and to think how they go on today about hygiene, health and safety, it has to make you smile. I never caught any diseases but I never liked the smell of those bins, I think I smelt like those bins.

As I was walking back to my house after we had fed the pigs, the men from the other family who kept pigs and their two sons were walking towards me, they shouted, "You've been taking our pig swill!"

"We have not," I said.

"Yes you have, you were seen and they told us it was you."

"Well, it wasn't me," I kept insisting.

"We will have the same amount back out of your bins next week, we have to feed our pigs as well you know," they shouted back. The man who kept the pigs whose swill we had taken went to see Dougie's dad about us taking his swill. Dougie got a good hiding and I was banned from going round to see the pigs or to collect the swill. It seemed that it was set in stone never to touch the other family's pig swill.

My mom kept the swill for that family but it was more than my life was worth to take my mom's pig swill. I was more afraid of my mom than any boy. Every Christmas the people who saved the swill all year were given a nice piece of pork to say thank you.

Enjoying watching the pigs while waiting for the pig swill to come to the boil. It was very interesting to see the pigs fight to get the best position when I poured the swill into the trough. After watching the pigs feed, I now know why my mom used to say to me at meal times you are like a pig in a trough.

60. MY TALKING BOOTS

I had run some errands for two neighbours and earned 9d (nine pennies), so one Saturday morning I decided to go to The Atlas Cinema on my own, Trevor was going with his mom to the Birmingham Rag Market. The cinema had its normal Saturday matinee at 12 noon (we always referred to it as the flicks) so I walked down Audley Road. I completely forgot about my right boot, the boots were the same ones I had from the *Birmingham Post and Mail*, the toe cap was flapping just like it was talking or singing 'There will always be an England'! It was hanging on by a thin piece of leather on the left-hand side where the toe cap had been ripped off. I was able to tuck that piece of leather inside my boot under my foot which made the boot look normal and the toe cap look okay. The trouble was I only took a few steps and it was flapping again, I patiently tucked in the leather strip to hold the toe cap in place constantly till I got to the flicks. How long I suffered that boot for I've no idea, I know I had to go to school like it, I don't recall any other children taking the mickey out of my boots.

They were showing Hopalong Cassidy that day at the cinema and I loved that cowboy with his black clothes and his silver accessories. At the end of the film we were like a herd of cattle all rushing to get to the bus stop first. I would normally walk home, but I must have been feeling lazy that afternoon, I had 2d (two pennies) left and it was only two stops so I waited for the bus. While I was standing there a boy standing next to me gave me a nudge with his elbow. I turned to see what he wanted, with a snigger and a sneer he said, "Your toe cap is flapping." I felt embarrassed and ashamed, I had completely forgotten about my boot.

"Why don't you get a pair of boots like mine," he sniggered all the time he was saying it, "mine are polished, why don't you polish yours?"

"My mom can't afford any polish at the moment, I'm getting some new ones next week," I said. I wasn't but I didn't know what else to say to him.

By this time there were lots of boys and girls waiting for the bus and they were all looking and laughing, I was praying for the bus to turn up, I even thought of running from the bus stop to get away from the humiliation I was suffering. Just as I was about to run, the bus turned up, I was so relieved. I went upstairs on the bus (I always went upstairs) and hid my feet under my seat so my boots were not seen. When I got off the bus, I must admit I was close to tears but I held them back. Where I came from boys were tough and never cried, at least not if anyone could see you, I grew up to believe that.

As I walked into our kitchen my mom could see I was upset, "What on earth's the matter, David?" she asked.

"Nothing, Mom," I replied.

"Yes there is, now what's up?" A mother knows her children well. I told her how the boy had laughed at me because the toe cap on my boot was flapping and all the boys and girls at the bus stop were also laughing at me. She hugged me and said, "You are better than all them, you would never take the rise out of anyone would you, son, that was in the same boat as you?"

"Never, Mom," I said (taking the rise meant taking the mick). I was taught to help people never to belittle anyone, if I had, which I never did, Mom would have belted me till I couldn't sit down, she was a stickler for good manners and respect. "I will ask your father when he comes home from work if he has any money to help me get you a pair of pumps."

I felt very happy at that moment, all I wanted was to look normal just like all the other children. I got my new pumps the next day and I felt really good walking around with footwear that looked okay. My thoughts were at that time, no one can take the rise out of me now, it's not good for children to feel this way, is it? But that's life because when those pumps got holes in the soles, which was not long because I had to wear them daily, they wore out very quickly and I was back to putting cardboard in them and tucking my socks under my feet. Life can be so cruel and hard even for children, for mothers even harder. I have the utmost respect for mothers they really do run the world.

I wish I'd had new boots then people wouldn't laugh at me.

61. FAGGOTS AND PEAS

Carmichaels was what everyone where I lived called the faggots and peas shop. Really it sold cooked meats like ham and pork, cheese, cereals, biscuits and all sorts of items, but Carmichaels were most well-known for their faggots and peas. People would queue for nearly an hour before they opened to buy their famous faggots and there would be as many as fifty people waiting. If you were at the front of the queue you got plenty of gravy, at the back of the queue you would definitely get no gravy, in fact many a time you got no faggots because they were sold out, so many a time I was sent to get in the queue early.

I would listen to people talking, not that I wanted to you understand, the times I heard about their daughters having babies and what a bad time they had. They would talk about someone dying and how they went about laying them out, I never liked to hear about people dying, but while in that queue on occasions I endured that type of conversation. I even heard about women's troubles and just about every disease known to man, in this case women!

We stood outside in winter and summer, it was a sight to see, some of the people (men and women) dressed to kill, some in slippers and aprons and Nora Batty style wrinkled stockings. Then there was scruffy little me usually needing a wash. Well, you can imagine it can't you, if you close your eyes and get a picture going in your mind's eye, I'm sure it will make you smile. The different utensils they would hold always fascinated me jugs, saucepans, big mugs and kettles (yes kettles!) people really did live on the edge of life in those days.

Some people would go to Suches, the hardware shop a couple of doors away to buy a basin or bowl (only if they were the better off type of people) which was always dusty and on occasions the shopkeeper would be asked to wash out the bowl which they kindly did with a smile.

This shop did quite a trade because of the faggots and peas. I tell you what, I'm proud to have been a part of it, it's part of my history those faggots and peas and they were the best I have ever tasted. Yes, I've tried the Black Country ones a few times, but they were not to my liking. Carmichaels have never been equalled in my humble opinion, the faggots were their own recipe, many people asked for the recipe but they always said, no.

One time I went to get some faggots for my mom I was at the back of the queue, I was supposed to get four faggots but because I messed about and was late, I only got three. The last three, I might add, with no gravy and it was raining so I got water in them. Well, I got a clip round the ear and no faggots for not doing as I was told.

62. ALL GROWN UP

The first time I ever wore long grey trousers with turn ups was in February, there was snow on the ground and it was very cold, they were really warm after wearing short trousers. When I went to school everyone noticed this scruffy boy had a new pair of trousers, which to me seemed wide and baggy, they took the mickey for the first morning and then it all faded away.

After school had finished and after I had my tea, I went with my two friends to Manor Park playing fields where there was quite a slope at the end of the football pitches. We had an old tin tray that we used for sledging down the slope, lots of children were there sledging. The posh kids had real sledges, not an old tin tray like we did, but we had every bit of much fun as they did. We were jealous of them if I'm honest, I always wanted a proper sledge but never got one. Mind you there were a lot of things I wanted and never got but that never ever stopped me enjoying life to the full. As a youngster I never found a sledge on the rubbish tip but I bet those posh kids never had the freedom of childhood that I had. I called every one that was better clothed than me, posh.

On the way home I looked down and saw a tear in my nice new trousers and they were dirty as well, I'd only had them for one day and I had already ruined them. Well, there was another good hiding coming my way. It's no wonder I was called 'Scruff' and a few other things I can't print. I can tell you when I was away from school and out with my friends I was in heaven I really was.

63. SIXPENCE FOR SWEETS

To go to the cinema in the 1940s and 1950s was a real treat. There were three types of certificate films: for a child to watch without an adult it was a U certificate; when it was an A a child always had to be accompanied by an adult and if it was an X certificate children were not allowed in at all. So it was U, A and X – I think it has all changed now.

Trevor and me used to stand outside the cinema, sometimes until it was too late to go in as the second picture had started and we would ask anyone to take us in. We would ask courting couples, old dears and people with children (thinking about it, it was rare to see a mom, dad and children going into the cinema at night). To the people I would say "take us in, Mister," or "take us in, Lady," and hold out my hand with the sixpence in it. We used to get a lot of comments, most I can't repeat, and those comments or insults only came from men never the ladies. The most common reply was of course was "No", usually quite loud.

When some kind person did say "Yes" I gave them my sixpence and was told to stand at the back of them so when we walked past the kiosk I wouldn't be seen with them. I must have looked a sight. Only once do I remember a couple allowing me to sit by them and I was told to keep quiet, don't fidget, sit still. I sat there frightened to death to move, well as you know children always fidget.

If you were sitting by yourself and there wasn't an adult either side of you and the picture was an A certificate, the usherette knew someone had taken you in and she would shine her torch on you and throw you out. They were cruel to children even when they were quiet and just enjoying the film, they would still throw them out. I found out years later that my eldest brother's sister-in-law was an usherette at the cinema, I was talking to her one day and asked if she ever regretted throwing kids out, she said, "No they shouldn't have been in the cinema." She was a hard woman.

When couples did take you in you were told, "We will take you in but you ain't sitting by us." Even now that thought makes me feel very uncomfortable, but of course I was very scruffy so I suppose I can't blame them. I remember the courting couples, the lady's hair was always nice and she wore bright red lipstick, the man had a smart suit and Brylcreemed hair, polished shoes and a smart tie. They looked happy and very much in love. Would you want a scruffy little kid sitting by you when you were in love? Neither would I (well, I'm not sure, I was that scruffy kid).

One evening I was standing there on my own, I can't remember why Trevor wasn't with me, asking, "take me in Lady?" when a pretty young lady with very dark shoulder-length hair, a three-quarter length coat and a scarf round her neck said, "Of course I will, Bab." I handed her my sixpence and to my surprise she said, "It's alright, Bab, I will pay for you. Go and buy some sweets for yourself."

I said, "Is it alright if I sit by you?"

"Of course you can," she replied. That never happened before and it never happened again. God bless that kind lady.

The next day I told Trevor, "A lady took me in and paid for me and I bought sweets with the sixpence." He was so jealous every time we stood outside the Atlas Cinema asking to be taken in, he would say, "Is this the lady that paid for you to be taken in?" He was hoping if we saw her, she would pay for us again, secretly so was I but, alas, I never saw her again.

It's wonderful remembering the past, even though it was hard, the small things we achieved made us very happy, as they do now.

64. PLAYING WITH FIRE

As children we all played together in the horse road, as my mom always called it, the girls played alongside of the boys and I very much liked to watch the girls skipping they were so fast and nimble. I tried a few times to join them but my feet were not fast enough, and it wasn't long before they told me to clear off because I was spoiling their game. I was quite good at hopscotch, though never good enough to beat the girls.

I had such wonderful times, those were wonderful years for all us children, we were poor and not well-clothed but when playing in the horse road with all our friends nothing else mattered. We were all good neighbours to one another and that combination can never be beaten, I don't care how rich or poor anyone is, with good friends and neighbours like I had, I was well off.

One day when we were playing in the road, one of the girls (I think it was Nanette, Trevor's sister) had a fire can which we were swinging around, I had a box of matches that I'd got from my mom's kitchen and I remember lighting the paper in the can. She swung it round till it got red hot and glowed, some of the girls were as tough as the boys. A girl named Ann said to me, "You shouldn't play with fire, nor should you have matches." So I remember I lit a match, I thought I would play her up and singe her hair, boy did I get scared. I never knew hair could burn the way it did, her hair went up in flames and Ann's sister Rita rushed over to her and put out the flames. I can't remember what Ann said to me, but we all carried on playing after I apologized to her. I remember that day well I never did anything I shouldn't after that day, with matches that is, for fear of it going wrong. Yes, I learnt a good lesson that day.

I still see Ann and her sister Rita from time to time, Rita like me loves talking about the past. Ann was playing one day with my sister Janet and a girl called June who lived two doors away from Ann, she had a blue ribbon in her hair. Ann said, "That's my ribbon you have in your hair, I lost it the other day."

June said, "No it is not, my mom bought it for me last week." I don't think Ann for one minute thought maybe she could be wrong. "Yes, it is," Ann replied, "I've got the other ribbon in the house that matches that one, I will go and get it," and she ran down the entry to the back of her house but when she was halfway down the entry, she tripped. I can still hear her screams to this day. She ripped open her top lip and damaged her two front teeth; her top lip is scarred but she is still a nice-looking lady.

All my friends that I grew up with are down-to-earth lovely people, it's wonderful to keep in touch with old friends and reminisce, it makes one appreciate old times and one's childhood.

65. DAD'S WORKS

When I was a boy most of the factories had Christmas parties for the children of their work force, they were great fun, as young children we loved them. It was very special for us to get jelly and blancmange, fruit, even cake, the icing on the cake, as the saying goes, was a present to take home after the party had ended.

My dad worked at the Metropolitan Camel and Carriage Works, they made trains. The factory was at the Gate, Saltley in Birmingham and I went there three times for the Christmas party. The present was sometimes a toy or a game, one year I got a gun, another year I got a Snakes and Ladders game, the third year I got a book and a compendium of games.

My dad left that firm for a short while and started to work for a firm called S U Carburettor. At the train works he was a radial driller, at his new company he was a labourer; why he left the train company I have no idea, yet he spent many years with that company. Anyway, I went twice to the Christmas parties at his new firm, I was given a colouring book both times as a present.

He left that firm after a couple of years or so and he returned to his old firm the Metropolitan Camel and Carriage Works, his boss was my mom's brother, my uncle Bob. At one Christmas party my sister Doreen got her present which was doll's furniture, she wasn't happy with it, she thought she was too old for it, so she got in the queue again. The man said, "You've been round before, haven't you?" "No," she replied, so he gave her another present. Did she moan, another set of doll's house furniture! Some girls had dolls, some had games and my sister wanted a game. That was the last Christmas party I ever went to at that firm and that year I got a red plastic water pistol gun.

My dad used to put on a show for all the children with my eldest brother, they always did the same play about school boys, they were very good.

My dad was a member of the British Legion, I went there a couple of times to their Christmas parties, the first time was after Christmas, they always had their Christmas parties after Christmas. The British Legion was at the back of my house, I got the coach outside the legion and we were taken to the Aston Hippodrome to see *Puss in Boots*, it was a wonderful show. We were given a bag with sweets, an apple and an orange in it, we got out of the coach and rushed in like a herd of cattle to get to what we thought would be the best seats in the hippodrome, boy we were noisy that afternoon! The apple was sour, I ate mine because I didn't waste food, I was grateful for my apple. The boy sitting next to me threw his apple, it hit a man on the back of his head and really hurt him, he was very angry, he was looking around hoping to see who had thrown it. I was thinking, I wish he had given me that apple. When the curtains went back it went very quiet, I was in heaven, that was the first and last time I went to a pantomime, I shall remember the song they sang at the end till the day I die, *This is the hour for us to say goodnight*. I was very moved by it, the colours, the atmosphere, it truly was electric and as I'm writing this I find I want to go again.

66. FIRE CANS

I have touched on fire cans in a previous chapter, this story was some time after the other one and tells a different tale. I loved playing with those fire cans, I realise now of course just how dangerous they were for young children to play with. If when on the tip I found a treacle tin (golden syrup) I would look for a nail and with a stone I would punch holes in it, I would then look for a piece of wire and twist the wire through a hole at the top of the can. I put paper and wood in it and lit the paper, then I would swing the can around till the wood was well and truly lit, I kept putting wood in until the can glowed red hot. I used to sort through the slack in the coal house, hoping my mom wouldn't catch me, coal made the can glow red hot really quickly.

My sister Doreen was swinging a can on our front garden one afternoon, "Dave!" she shouted, "come here and pick this piece of wood up for me."

"Can I have a go then?" I asked.

"If you go into the coal house and sort through the slack for some lumps of coal," she answered.

"If I do, then can I have a go?" I pleaded.

"Yes okay, but only if you find a lot," she replied. So, into the coal house I went and came out looking blacker than the coal, with the whitewash off the walls all down my back. Doreen was very pleased with the amount that I had found, after putting it in the can and getting it glowing very hot after she had swung it around a few times I said, "Can I have a go now?" Doreen again asked me to pick the wood up that lay not far from her feet, I bent down to pick up the wood and as she was swinging the glowing red hot can around it hit me over my left eye and split it wide open. Off to the hospital I went with Mom to have it stitched. On returning home Doreen was given a good hiding and fire cans were banned, never to be seen again, not anywhere near our house anyway. I loved to hear the swishing sound as the cans were being swung around and seeing how they looked in the dark, glowing red and how bright the sparks looked when flying out of the can. I was not so keen when my left eye got split open!

Making our fire cans glow in the dark.

67. HEADING HOUSE BRICKS

There was an alleyway at the rear of the shops just up the road from my house, it was the delivery access for the shops. One morning walking to the shops with Trevor, we noticed a builder's lorry parked in the alley, a builder was working on the walls surrounding the backyards of the shops. We could hear all the banging, rubble being thrown onto the back of the lorry, quick as a flash as the saying goes, I said, "Come on, Trev, we might be able to earn some money." Climbing over the rubble without any thought of danger I said to the builder, "Excuse me, Mister, do you want any help?" "Yes, lads, would you start to throw all the bricks onto the back of the lorry?"

"Yes, easy," I said.

"Good, you start there," he said, pointing to the entrance of the yard. "Nice and steady," I said to Trevor, "if we make it last, we might be able to come tomorrow and earn more money." We worked really well together and before long we had cleared the whole entrance.

All was going well when our friend Johnny shouted, "Hey, what's going on? How did yo' get this job?"

"We asked if he needed any help and he said yes," I answered. "How much is he paying ya?" asked Johnny.

"He never said," I replied.

"I'm going to ask him if I can help," Johnny said.

The builder said, "You three get in a line I will throw the bricks to you, then you," he said pointing at Trevor, "can throw them onto the lorry." All was going well, we must have moved seven or eight hundred bricks, the ends of our fingers were very sore by this time. I threw a brick to Trevor but because his fingers were sore, he dropped it and I didn't turn quick enough to say to Johnny don't throw any more bricks, as I turned a brick that Johnny had thrown hit me on the head just above my

158

right eye brow, the blood cascaded down my face. The builder came rushing over, I put my finger over the cut, "I'm alright!" I shouted, "don't touch me." I couldn't stand people messing with me when I had been hurt (I'm still the same now).

"I think I can manage on my own now, lads," the builder said, "thanks for your help." Not a penny did we receive, we had worked for nothing. When I stopped bleeding I said, "Well Trev, now we ain't earned any money because of Johnny lets go see if any of our ladies wants any errands doing." So we knocked on a couple of doors but no luck. By this time my eye was really swollen and painful and I said to Trevor, "Trev I'm not feeling good I'm going home."

My mom said, "Oh no, not again. What have you been up to now?" "It's okay mom I got hit by a house brick helping a man at the back of the shops." With a quick look at it, Mom said, "You silly little bugger, you will be the death of me yet."

"Sorry, mom." That's all I could think of to say, I lay on the settee and went to sleep for a long time, how long I've no idea but it was dark when I woke up. I never cleaned that cut, I had a beautiful big lump the next morning and a lovely black eye as well, my eye was very sore for a week afterwards. Mind you it never stopped me running errands for the ladies so I could earn a few pennies.

68. THE QUEEN

Coming up to Bonfire night, about a week before really, me and Trevor went around the area of Castle Bromwich looking for firewood for our bonfire. Well we found these two big branches which were quite heavy and we dragged them past Bradford Hall, which we all thought was haunted. Facing the Hall were two rows of what I think were Chestnut trees, I think the owner of the hall had those trees planted so when he looked out of his window he looked down the avenue of trees, we called it the conker woods.

Anyway me and Trevor were pulling those branches along this avenue of trees when we came to the main Chester Road, you can imagine how dirty and scruffy we were. Nearly by the Chester Road, I couldn't believe my eyes, there were lots of people waving the English flag and union jacks. To my surprise the Queen was passing! I shouted as I ran towards the road dragging my branch, "Hi Queenie!" Well, she laughed as I waved and shouted, we were very close to her. I wonder what she thought when she saw two dirty scruffy kids from Birmingham pulling two big tree branches behind them. I will never forget seeing the Queen laugh at Trevor and me.

I bet if the authorities had known we were there looking like that we would have been hidden away or cleaned up. That's my claim to fame and at least it gave the Queen a laugh. I think that was the day she opened All Saints Church at Shard End. That's the church I was married at because my girlfriend lived at Shard End and then you had to get married in the parish where your intended came from and that was Shard End.

Me and Trevor waving to the Queen as she passed, her head went back as she laughed when she saw two dirty little urchins dragging branches for their bonfire. She was on her way to open All Saints Church in Shard End, Birmingham, in the 1950s.

Bradford Hall is the building in the background. Trevor and I were dragging branches one bonfire night, as we approached the Chester Road we saw the Queen.

Chester Road where we saw the Queen.

69. A PENNY FOR HIM

At the start of one November, I called for my friend Trevor and said, "Hey, Trev, I have had a great idea."

"Oh yeah? What have I got to do now?"

"Well, Trev, I thought if I dress you as Guy Fawkes and sit you in a pushchair, I can push you to the bus stop up the road by the shops, you can hold a cup in your hand, I will stand at the side of you and ask for a penny for the guy."

"I like that idea, Dave."

"Can you get a pair of your dad's old trousers, Trev?"

"I can get my dad's old overcoat and his flat cap."

"If we go round the back of the corn shop (this shop was called Turners) there is usually a lot of straw on the floor by their back gate where they have their deliveries. We could go and pick it up and use it to put in your trouser legs, in the sleeves of your coat and out of the cap. Then we need to find some string to tie round the bottom of the trousers to hold the straw in and round the sleeves, we can put the straw under your arms."

"Okay," said Trevor, "let's do it." If my memory serves me right I dressed him up and I think I blacked his face with coal dust. I stood outside the bus stop with him holding his cup for the pennies, we didn't do very well, only collecting 7d. So, I had the bright idea of going around the houses after we had had our tea. I told Trevor I ain't pushing yo' in the pushchair, yo' can walk with me, I will ask for a penny for the guy and you just stand there. This we did, I knocked on lots of doors and asked for a penny for the guy. We got lots of different comments! Some would have a good laugh and give us 2d, some would tell us to clear off, but the main comment was, "Sod off, you bloody little scroungers." Or words to that effect.

One house I remember going to was where the man that ran our post office lived, he looked at us laughed and said, "Which one of you is the guy?" I looked at him puzzled and said, "He is," pointing at Trevor. Still laughing, he said, "I was only making sure." Then he gave me two shillings. As we walked up his path I said to Trevor, "I wonder why he never knew which was the guy, Trev?"

"Dunno, Dave," Trevor replied. Talk about being thick.

Nothing deterred us, we were used to adults insulting us and we used the money we got to go swimming or to go to the flicks (the cinema) and of course we would buy sweets. My favourites sweets at that time were sherbet lemons, they had sherbet in the middle of them. Funny thing is I can't stand them now.

We also used the money that we collected to go roller-skating. Trevor's brother Tony came with us and we always had great fun. There were lots of rough boys that went to the roller rink, so I think they had about three bouncers, I saw many a lad thrown out of there and I mean thrown. I mostly stayed in the middle of the rink, that's where all us wimps went. Yes, I was a wimp! When there were six or more kids holding hands, the kid on the end would be flipped round at such a speed it was very dangerous. I was knocked flying a couple of times by the one on the end of the line, he couldn't stop, I even saw kids hit the barrier and get knocked out because of the speed they were travelling and some got really bad cuts. They only did this when they thought the bouncer wasn't around because it wasn't allowed and was stopped as soon as the bouncers saw it start. Everyone that was in the line would get thrown out. I think when they were ready to go home because they had had enough of roller skating that's when they did the line-up, there is a name for it but I'm afraid I can't call it to mind.

One afternoon when Tony, Trevor and I had earned enough money from Guy Fawkes-ing, we went to the skating rink. When they gave me my pair of skates the lace was half missing in the one skate. I took it back to complain but even the ladies behind the counter were as rough as the bouncers, so I was told to clear off and make do. At the end of that

Trevor and I loved doing the things none of our friends would do and me dressing Trevor up as Guy Fawkes was, I think, one of them.
We had fun, Trevor and I.

session, which I think was an hour, some lads from the previous session didn't hand their skates back in and left them lying around because they had sneaked out of the side doors. So, I decided to take a lace from one of the boots and put it in my boot, when a bouncer came up to me, grabbed hold of me by the scruff of the neck and accused me of trying to steal the skates. He was shaking me violently and threatening to get the police, bear in mind I was only a young whippersnapper of about nine. I was almost in tears as I tried to explain that I was only replacing the lace because the one that I had been given was not long enough and I had asked the lady at the counter but she refused to change the boots. He frog-marched me to the counter to find out if what I was saying was the truth and the lady confirmed what I was saying. The bouncer said, "Sorry, son. But we do lose a lot of skates from people stealing them." I said, "I love coming here, Mister, I love to skate." Then in a very stern voice he said, "Do not ever do it again, I shall remember you and if I find you in here and you are taking laces out of the skates, even if you have paid, I will still throw you out and you will not get a refund. Do you understand?" "Yes, Sir," I said as I was cowering and looking at the floor. I wonder how those type of places would get on these days with the new generation.

That roller rink was off the Golden Hillock Road in Small Heath. It was actually in Warf Road and we went there many, many times. We always walked from our houses in Glebe Farm which was a very long walk, about ten miles even more I reckon, all to save bus fares. It was eventually turned into a bingo hall and when I worked for Coca Cola I had to deliver to that building, the first time I made a delivery there I had a look around at the interior. The memories that came back to me were wonderful memories, then I remembered that bouncer and that half a lace, it was an exciting time for me all those years ago. I believe it's now been demolished.

70. BLOOD, SWEAT AND TEARS

One morning Trevor and I sat on the garden wall in my front garden and put our brains together (which were very few as neither of us could read or write very well) to find a way of making money. We had some hare-brained ideas and digging out a drive was most definitely one of them.

We went to our local community centre to ask if they needed any jobs doing, I was off school getting over a cold and I can't remember why Trevor was off school. We knocked on the door at the community centre and a man opened it, "Do you want any jobs doing, Mister?" I asked. The first thing he said was, "Why are you not at school?"

"We are getting over a cold," I explained to him.

"Oh, I see," he said. As I turned to walk away after he had told us he didn't require any jobs doing, I spotted through a half-opened door at the end of the corridor a snooker table so I asked if we could play on it. "Yes you can," he said to my great surprise, "so long as you are very quiet."

"Thank you, Mister," we both said together.

About an hour had passed when the man came into the room where we were. "I say, you boys, are you interested in gardening?" Without a second's thought I said, "Yes we like gardening we do it all the time." We knew absolutely nothing about gardening, my mind was in overdrive wondering how much money we could make. "I live in Castle Bromwich, do you know where that is?" he asked. Well, of course we didn't know.

I replied, "We will find it, Mister, if you give us directions."

"Tell you what, boys, I will leave early tonight and take you in my car and show you the way. Is that all right, boys?"

"Yes, Mister," Trevor said very quickly.

"Okay, boys, you carry on playing snooker." We were there from about ten or ten-thirty in the morning till late afternoon with nothing to eat we just drank water from a tap in the toilet.

"Wow, Trev, a ride in a car!" We were excited I can tell you. We got into his car, it smelt of leather I can still smell that to this very day, it was an Austin. "Boys, you will have to walk back, it's not that far only I have to go out as soon as I've shown you the job." "That's okay, Mister, we like walking don't we, Trev?"

"Yeah." We would say anything to earn money and to get a ride in a car, we didn't know anyone with a car. I was ten, Trevor was eleven and we thought he was a millionaire because he had a car. As we were going along the road, I was hoping to see one of our friends so we could wave to them, they would have been ever so jealous but we never passed one of them, well they would have been at home having their tea.

We arrived at his house and he parked the car on the road. "Here we are boys, this is what I want you to do, I want this hawthorn hedge taking down and this sandstone wall. I have a wheelbarrow you can use to take the stones round the back, right to the bottom of the garden and the hawthorn hedge you can drag round the back. When you have done that, I want the soil digging out and again barrowing round the back to the bottom of the garden but keep all the items separate so it will be easy for me to move at a later date. The reason for doing this, boys, I want to put my car on my garden to keep it off the road. Do you think you can manage it boys?" he asked. Trevor and me stood by the wall with the hedge on top of it, it must have been nine foot or more high and for a ten and an eleven-year-old this was a mammoth task. "Can you start tomorrow, boys? I want it done as quick as possible."

"Yes, Mister," I replied.

Next morning it was nice and warm, we walked from our houses to Castle Bromwich, it must have been five miles or more and it took us about thirty-five minutes to walk there. As we walked up the path the lady of the house came out to us, "There you are, boys, I've put out the tools ready for you, mind you clean them when you have finished with them. There is a spade, a saw and a pair of secateurs." What are those? I thought to myself, I've never heard of them. "And here is a lump hammer," she explained, "it's for knocking the wall down and the barrow is round the back when you need it." I asked for a drink of water before we started, hoping she would give us pop, we got what I asked for – water.

We started to cut down the hawthorn hedge, we didn't know it had thorns, so we got scratched and both of us ripped our arms to bits. It took us all day to dig and cut up that hedge, I was, by this time, very tired, so was Trevor. We stopped work at 4.30pm, I remember that because the lady came out with a glass of home-made Ginger Beer and a fairy cake each. It was the best Ginger Beer I've ever tasted but that might be because I was tired, hot, thirsty and very hungry. We only had two glasses of Ginger Beer and two fairy cakes all day. The lady next door asked the lady we were working for the time, that's how I remember it was 4.30pm. We had left most of the hedge lying on the front garden ready to put round the back next morning.

We arrived home worn out. "Trev, it's harder than I thought it would be."

"It is, Dave, ain't it? Shall we not go tomorrow?"

"Let's see how we feel in the morning," I said. After a good night's sleep, yes I died as soon as my head hit the pillow, the next morning I had two pieces of toast and a cup of tea and I was feeling okay. I called for Trevor and he like me was feeling refreshed after a night's sleep he said, "Right, Dave, let's go, we won't let it beat us, will we?"

"No way Trev," I replied sticking out my chest like I was Charles Atlas. We worked in the only set of clothes we possessed, our seven-days-a-week suit! We were not very clean, our clothes that is, well I did wash my face.

On arriving we took what was left of the hedge around to the back garden, it must have been 80 yards long, it could have been less but to a youngster it seemed very long. Then we started to take down the sandstone wall, it took us two days. I was pushing the wheelbarrow, I grew tired very quick pushing the barrow with big stones in it, so I ended up putting one stone at a time in. After the hedge and wall were down, we started to dig out the soil which we found to be the hardest job. Many, many barrow loads – we took just over a week to complete the job, without a doubt it was far too

*This is the drive that Trevor and I dug out in the
Castle Bromwich area of Meriden.*

big a job for two little urchins like us, Trevor and I found it to be too much for us both at times. Our clothes were more ruined than they were before.

We cleaned up, put all the tools away, "Cor, Trev, I wonder how much he will pay us?" Out came the lady with two glasses of Ginger Beer and two fairy cakes. "Well done, boys, my husband will be pleased, you have worked very hard. He'll be home soon, I've phoned him to tell him you have finished the drive."

We had great expectations, saying to each other ten shillings each, well at least eight shillings. We were sitting on the wall on the other side of the garden when Trevor said, "Here he is, Dave." We knew it was his car because not one other car passed us all day, only the milkman and the baker and they both had horse drawn carts. He drove his car onto his drive for the first time, got out of the car, and with his hands on hips looked up and down his new drive. He said, "Wonderful, wonderful, boys. Thank you very much you have worked really hard, you should be very proud of yourselves." He said, "Thank you very much," again, shook our hands and said, "anytime you want to play snooker you come and see me," he turned, walked into the house and closed the door. I looked at Trevor, we were both in shock. "He will come out in a minute and pay us, Dave."

"Yeah of course he will." Wrong, he never showed his face, we waited a good fifteen minutes all that work for glasses of Ginger Beer and fairy cakes. "In future, Trev, I'm going to ask how much they will pay before we start work."

"Yeah, I will too, Dave."

Every time I pass that house in my car, I say to whoever is with me, "Me and Trevor dug that drive out."

"We know, you have told us before," they always reply. One day as we were passing that drive, my wife said, "I know you and Trevor dug out that drive." I laughed.

She said, "Dave, why don't you write it down and put it in a book then you won't need to tell me again that you and Trevor dug out that drive." So I have, that's how come you are reading about it now. The trouble is I've nothing to talk about now!

71. BIRMINGHAM HIPPODROME

Trevor's brother Tony and I went to the Atlas Cinema, again I have no idea why Trevor wasn't with us as the three of us went out together on many occasions. Whenever we went swimming it was the three of us, which was quite often in those days and as time went by we went with my sister Janet and Trevor's sister Nannette to Woodcock Street baths. Trevor swam nineteen lengths of that swimming baths, it was near Birmingham city centre. Any road up, while I was watching the film Tony suddenly said, "Dave, look what I've just found – a wage packet." When he opened it, there to his amazement, was fifty shillings inside it. Tony gave me the ten-shilling note. Boy, did I feel rich!

We left the cinema and got the number 14 bus to Birmingham city centre and walked around the town for a while. Tony asked, "Ay Dave, have you ever been to the Birmingham Hippodrome?"

"Cor no," I replied.

"Okay, come on then you're in for a treat." So in we went for the last performance of the day. David Hughes, the singer was appearing, I waved to him and Tony looked at me, laughed and said, "Why are you waving to a man?" I felt such a fool! After the singer, Morecambe and Wise came on (I think it was them, whoever it was I liked them) and when the show was over I got David Hughes' autograph. That was the first time I had heard of him.

When I got married, I gave my autograph book to my wife's two little brothers but they ripped it up. It had contained all my school friends' wishes to me and their signatures on the day I left school. I really miss that book, that's one of the reasons I'm writing down all my memories. I can then at least read through it to jog my memory as the years pass and my memory fades. But the main reason I've written it is for my children to know how their dad was brought up and lived and the things I have done throughout my life, it may even be of interest to my grandchildren as they grow older.

72. THE COAL MERCHANTS

One warm summer's day, around nine o'clock in the morning, I walked to the tip as I usually did, looking for old shoes for my mom to burn on the fire. I know it was summer but the summer evenings were sometimes chilly, any road up the old shoes were saved for those chilly nights. The reason we had no coal was because my mom would pay weekly for the coal but she fell behind with the payments so the coal merchants would not let her have any more coal until the bill was paid in full. It was a treat when, finally, I watched with much interest the coalman carrying a hundred weight of coal through the kitchen to what my mom called the coal 'ole (a cupboard under the stairs).

One thing has always stuck in my mind and it always used to puzzle me as a young lad, was why my mom (never my dad) used to whitewash the coal 'ole walls. I would be sent to the hardware shop to ask for a ball of chalk and a washing blue cube. The ball of white would be broken up in a bucket, filled up with cold water, then the blue would be added. The boiler stick that my mom used for getting clothes out of the boiler after being washed would be used for stirring, until all was dissolved. That stick was also used a few times on my backside when I played up. Then with a large brush the walls were whitewashed, it would be brushed onto the three walls, all very wet and messy I seem to remember.

As I said, what puzzled me was when the coalman went to tip the coal from the bag that was on his back, my mom would say, "I've whitewashed the walls, don't dirty them." The poor coalman would try so hard to keep the coal from hitting the walls, as if his job wasn't hard enough, but he did what he was told and said, "I haven't dirtied your walls, Mrs Prosser." He knew my mom, he only lived a few doors away from our house. A thought just came to me, every time I went to get some coal from the coal 'ole the white chalk would come off the walls and make a real mess of my clothes, so sometimes when the coal was low it was a real struggle to get the coal without getting the whitewash on my clothes.

The house the coalman lived in was number 38 the same number as our house but his house was in Swancote Road just round the corner from our house. I remember Mom talking one day to my dad and saying that we should have had the house the coalman lived in but there was a mix-up at the council office because both houses had the same number. She had asked the coalman at the time to swap houses but he wouldn't swap, he said he was happy with his house. My mom always said she preferred the coalman's house. I think our house, which was a semi-detached on a corner, was far better than the coalman's house which was a terraced house with an entry for access to the back garden, at least we had our own back gate giving us access without having to go through the front door. Mind you, the coalman's house had a back gate but they had to share the entry plus it backed onto my school so the noise level was bad when the children were out in the playground.

73. 2/- TO SPEND

I found as I was growing up that girls were the cruellest creatures on God's green earth. I suppose when one is poorly dressed, even scruffy looking, it would make girls not want to be near you or touch you. It started in the infants when we had dancing lessons – all the girls would say, "I'm not dancing with you." I was usually left out on my own, you would have thought the teacher would have noticed this and made a girl dance with me. Mind you, I hated dancing with the girls and on the odd occasions I did dance with a girl, they would say, "Don't touch me, just pretend to be holding me."

One time the teacher did make me put my arms around a girl, she made me feel like I was something she had trodden in, as soon as the teacher turned away, she jumped backwards and literally shuddered and said, "I hate you touching me, you are scruffy." I think that has hurt me more in life than anything else I can think of, apart from the time when I went to Weston-super-Mare and couldn't buy my mom a present. I remember the tune we danced to, even now I can hear it while I am writing this book it went, step close, step close, step close, step lar la la… I'm sure you know the rest. I just wanted it to end. I always felt very uncomfortable in that lesson, well all lessons really, but I hated that dancing lesson. All through school I had that treatment off girls they just did not like sitting by me, they even asked the teacher to move me away from them.

The seniors was a whole new ball game, those teachers had a licence to bully children, we thought we were grown-up but we were still children. I can still remember the afternoon we were taken across from the juniors to the seniors to meet the headmaster, as we were going into the seniors after the summer holidays. We were sat in rows in the main hall, on the floor, and in walked Mr Bradbury the headmaster of the seniors and for some unknown reason, I can see that afternoon like it was yesterday, his first words were, "Good afternoon, boys and girls, you are the big boys and girls of the juniors, after the holidays you will be the little boys and girls of the seniors." That thought sent a shiver down my back, I've no idea why.

Where have the years gone? My mom told me many times enjoy your childhood son it's the best years of your life. How right you were, Mom so that is exactly what I did.

74. BAGS OF RAGS

It was great to be young and to have the freedom me and Trevor had and the friends I grew up with. Trevor and me did the most things together, our other friends got pocket money every week, not much, but more than us at that time.

We had an idea, well it was Trevor's idea really, to go all around our neighbours and ask if they had any old rags or woollens they didn't want. Talk about cheek, we knew no boundaries and we had no nerves at all, we would do anything to earn money. Most people were kind to us and we were very surprised at the amount we were given because most people in those days wore their clothes till they were threadbare just like we did, plus they could have given them to the rag and bone man and got a baby chick or a gold fish. After we filled two sacks up and sorted the woollens from the rags, we were surprised to find better clothes in there than the ones we were wearing, to be honest we swapped our clothes for ones we had been given as rags. We both now had a new set of clothes and we felt good, even though we never got them washed, well that never bothered Trevor and me, we were used to living in a world of make-do-and-mend. Funny thing was Mom never noticed my clothes were different, if she did, she never mentioned it.

A boy came up to me one day and took the rise out of me, "That was my jumper, we threw it away because it's got a stain under the arm." He pulled back my coat (that had also been someone else's), "See, I told you it was mine. You two are scroungers and scruffy." It was at that moment I realised I wished I was a bully just like he was, me and Trevor were nice gentle boys. I took off that jumper and threw it back in the ragbag, found another jumper from the rag bag and wore that (me and Trevor could have won a fancy-dress competition without even getting changed!).

We carried our sacks of rags from Glebe Farm all the way to Cuckoo Bridge to an area known as Aston to the firm we called Raggy Allan's.

It took us one and a half hours to walk it, we walked along the number 14 bus route past the Fox and Goose, through Washwood Heath then to Aston. The man with the scales would weigh the rags first, then the woollens and he would say, "Look, boys, that's what they weigh." I would look but I hadn't a clue what I was looking at. "Yes," I would say. He wrote the weight down on a ticket, we then walked past a mountain of rags on either side of us to an office that looked like it belonged in Dickensian times. A glass window was slid open, we handed a faceless person our ticket, and out came a hand with our money in it.

We did that walk many times to sell our rags, the ones in the sacks I might add, not the ones we were wearing. We used the money for swimming, bus fares and a cup of Cow & Gate after swimming at Woodcock Street baths. We earned our own money so I think we should feel a little proud of ourselves.

75. PLAYING GAMES

Me and my friends played games every spare minute we had when we were not running errands, there were six of us and we played every evening in the summer time. I loved the warm summer evenings, the energy we had was endless, we were very fit little fellows. It's only when one gets older you realise just how fit you were and if I had half that energy now I would be happy, mind you I was very fit till I reached my sixties so I should be grateful it's now my turn to be old.

These are the games I liked most of all:

Polly on the Mopstick
Two teams of equal amounts. If there were eight of us, we all lined up and we would pick two captains then find an object like a piece of wood or a stone and make one side heads and the other side tails, as none of

Polly on the Mopstick.

179

us had any money. The winning captain would have first pick of the people lined up, we did this for many types of games. To be a Mopstick team the leader bends over holding onto the fence with the rest of the team bending forward holding on to the waist of the person in front. The Pollys would run and jump on to the backs of the Mopsticks to try and collapse them. The leader of the Mopstick had to shout, "Polly on the Mopstick 1, 2, 3!" and win the game. If the Mopstick hadn't collapsed when this was shouted, they were the winners and the Pollys had to become the Mopsticks. Thinking back now this was a very dangerous game to play it's a wonder none of us had a broken back.

Kick the Can

This was the same as hide and seek the only difference was whichever one was on first, he or she had to find the ones hiding. We always played this game in the dark. When the ones hiding thought he or she couldn't be seen they would kick the can and then they would run and hide again without being spotted. If the person on saw whoever kicked the can, they would shout that person's name and then they would be on if it was correct.

British Bulldog

If any game was dangerous it was this one. Again, an object would be used for heads and tails to see who would be the Bulldog. Standing on the side of the pavement would be the rest of us, the Bulldog would stand in the middle of the road, our road was laid in concrete, this was in squares so the lines where the concrete finished were the boundaries. Now the Bulldog would shout the name of the person he wished to tackle and that person had to try to get past the Bulldog and get to the other side of the road, but you weren't allowed to run until the Bulldog shouted "British Bulldog". When the Bulldog tackled you, if he got you down on the ground and shouted "British Bulldog!" it would be your turn to be the Bulldog. We got a few scratches and bruises trying to get to the other side of the road.

One evening a boy named Derek, who never ever played with us asked if he could play, he lived at the top end of my road, he was very

This is how we played British Bulldog in the road.

well dressed. "What about your clothes?" I said. "I don't care," he said, "I want to play." "Okay you can play," Billy said. Billy was the Bulldog after two of us had got past Billy, he called out Derek's name and made him wait a while so Derek's adrenaline would be pumping. Billy shouted "British Bulldog!" and Derek almost got past him. Billy dived at Derek, got his hands round Derek's legs and he went down, hitting his head on the gutter and splitting his head wide open. The blood flew everywhere and off he ran home. We were told he had lots of stitches and he never played with us again. Funny to think about it now, we played that game for many a year and scratches were the worst we ever got.

King of the Hill
This was exactly the same as British Bulldog, the only difference was it was played on a hill covered in grass we could be as rough as we liked on grass.

Hot Rice

Where the names for these games came from, I have no idea. We all stood in a ring with clenched fists, using a tennis ball which was thrown from a clenched fist and caught with a clenched fist. If when thrown to you, you dropped the ball you were on and as soon as the ball was dropped everyone would run. The person that was on had to throw the ball and try to hit the ones running away, some of the boys threw the ball too hard, it really hurt. If you were hit it was your turn to be on and you had to throw and try to hit someone with the ball, if you sat on a fence or a gate with your feet off the ground the ball could not be thrown at you. We would lie on the floor with our feet in the air and the thrower would stand poised, waiting for your feet to touch the ground, there was a time limit that your feet could be off the ground. That's how it went but time is fading the memory somewhat on that part of the game.

Gutter Cricket

Played with four sticks of wood or lollipop sticks, these were placed in the gutter with three up right and one across the top, the same as wickets in cricket. When the ball was thrown, if the sticks were knocked down it became the same as hot rice, great fun! It's a shame we had to grow up – but my children say I never did.

Famous Stars' Initials

This game we played on an old bike. We would ride around in circles saying the first letters of the name of the star to the people standing on the pavement who had to guess the name of the star. Whoever guessed the name first got on the bike and rode around in circles, they then had to think of a star's name. The most common ones used were DD (Donald Duck or Diana Dors), MM (Mandy Miller or Marilyn Monroe, Micky Mouse wasn't allowed), NW (Norman Wisdom), WH (Will Hay) or OMR (Old Mother Riley). We played for hours, boy we had lots of energy and a lifetime of fun.

I Wrote a Letter to my Wife

We all stood around in a circle facing inwards, one person stood outside the circle and ran around the outside of the circle, the people in the circle would be singing "I wrote a letter to my wife and on the way, I dropped it," when the words "dropped it" were said, as the runner passed you, you looked behind you to see if the letter had been dropped by your feet. You weren't allowed to look until the person had passed you. In our case the letter was any item we had at that time, normally it would have been a handkerchief, but most times it was a piece of rag. If it had been dropped behind you, you had to pick it up and catch the person that had dropped it before they got back to the space where you had been standing. If they didn't catch you, they had to keep running and the singing would start all over again. I loved that game. All the children I grew up with were wonderful. The rhyme we used to sing when we were playing this game was:

> "I wrote a letter to my wife and on the way, I dropped it,
> Somebody must have picked it up and put it in their pocket.
> Thief, thief, drop it, drop it, thief, thief drop it, drop it."

True, Dare, Kiss or Promise

I liked this game it was a good laugh. *True* you were asked something that they knew about you just to see if you would tell the truth, usually they would ask who you were in love with. *Dare* of course meant you were dared to do silly things like diving over a high hedge or surprising one of the girls and telling them you loved them. If you said *Kiss*, then you were told who to kiss, if you refused you had to do a forfeit and the person who was on at that time would tell you to do something really daft like kiss the floor or take your shoes off and run through a puddle. *Promise* you were told to make a promise, if you didn't keep it, they would think of something horrible to do to you, like get you in trouble with your mom or a neighbour. We really did have some great times playing this game. Oh, to be young again.

Football

When we were playing football one day outside Johnny's house, I kicked the ball and it came off the side of my foot and smashed a window in Johnny's house. I had to pay 6d (sixpence every week) till I paid for it, I ran errands to save the money up. I was very careful after that.

Playing my favourite game – Football.

THINK OF A NUMBER BELOW TEN
(DON'T TELL ME WHAT IT IS)

DOUBLE IT, ADD FOUR, HALVE IT, TAKE AWAY
THE FIRST NUMBER YOU THOUGHT OF,
YOU ARE LEFT WITH NUMBER 2

Do you remember this puzzle? Everyone did these types of puzzles. DID YOU?

76. ONE IN THE EYE

One very cold winter's day, me and my friends were playing in the horse road. The snow had started to melt but was still sort of frozen – when rolled in the hands it was snow mixed with ice and water ran through our fingers when we rolled a snow ball. We all agreed we wouldn't throw this mixture of snow and ice at each other, only at cans or objects that we stood up on the hedge.

I had been sliding down the hill and after an hour my feet were soaking so I said, "Lads, I'm going in to dry and warm my feet. I can't feel my toes."

"Yo wimp!" they shouted.

"It's alright for yo your feet ain't wet and frozen like mine," I said. So Billy decided to start throwing those ice snowballs at me.

"Come on, Billy!" we all shouted, "we've agreed we wouldn't throw the ice it's dangerous."

He was laughing, "Come on you girls, I thought yo were tough boys."

"Now look, Billy," I was saying, as I turned round to look at him an ice ball hit me in both eyes. The pain was unbearable, I thought I had lost my sight. All my mates shouted, "Billy yo idiot, you've blinded Dave!"

Billy was really frightened. I was without my eyesight for about nine days. I had to go to hospital with my mom, all because Billy couldn't resist throwing snowballs. I was off school for two weeks, it could have been three, and when I returned to school I was taken to the headmaster's office, well frog-marched would be the right way to describe it. I was poked and pushed.

"Why weren't you at school?" I was so scared my mind went blank, I just could not think straight.

"Well? Well? Answer me!"

Because I hesitated, he was shouting, "Trying to think up a story are we?" When I suddenly remembered the icy snowball Billy had thrown at me.

"A snow ball was thrown at me, Sir and hit me in the eyes I went blind for a few days."

"Well that's a good one, did you rehearse that story before you came into my office?"

"No, Sir," I replied.

"You are a liar." Nothing I said would be believed.

"You think I'm stupid don't you? Snowballs in your eyes, you were playing truant weren't you?" the headmaster was really shouting at me.

"No, Sir," I answered.

"Don't you 'No, Sir' me, my lad," the head went on at me.

"Go on get out of my office you are a waste of time!" he shouted at me as he pushed me towards the door, it really upset me. I never had days off school for no reason, I would have but I was more scared of my mom than any teacher. I had really suffered with my eyes. That's one of the reasons I hated going to school, I got into trouble for no good reason with those teachers. The art teacher, Miss Parry put me in detention every day for two weeks, "Why, Miss? Miss I haven't done anything."

"Well you will go to detention tomorrow as well now!" she shouted. The boy behind me was talking so she again gave me detention, I said nothing for fear of getting more detention.

77. MINE OR YOUR MOM'S

It's hard to imagine that these days a family of six (four children and two adults) could be living in a house with no food in the house, not even a crust of bread to eat or any coal or wood to burn to heat the house. That's how we lived for many a year. There were times of course when we would seem to have enough to eat but not often enough, I don't think.

In the 1950s almost everyone got paid on a Friday, but Trevor's dad Fred got paid on a Thursday, he worked in the wholesale fruit market in the centre of Birmingham. Well, my mom used to make me look out of the living room window to tell her when Fred was coming down the road. "He's coming, Mom!" I would shout.

"Give him five minutes to get into the house then go and ask him if he will lend me 2/6d (that's half a crown)." He always lent my mom money on a Thursday and after I took the money back to my mom, she would send me up the road to the shops for a loaf, potatoes and sometimes Spam, that was the cheapest meat at that time from Braggs the cake shop.

Some of my relatives worked for Mr Bragg during the war, one of them being my Auntie Maggie. Being so short of sugar she helped herself and took sugar home in her handbag, so Mr Bragg went to my granddad and asked him to have a word with his daughter and tell Maggie to stop stealing the sugar. Granddad was none too pleased as he was unaware of what had been going on.

My Auntie Maggie was killed during a bombing raid, I would like to have known her. The family lived at number 53 Ash Road in Saltley and when they were bombed out they moved to number 20. Auntie Maggie was killed on the 10th of April 1941, she was only 34 years of age.

It wasn't always doom and gloom, sometimes life seemed wonderful. I think maybe the winters were the hardest times, more coal had to be bought and burnt, extra gas was used and we seemed to eat more in the winter. One Thursday I went to borrow 10/- for my mom and Trevor's dad said, "I'm not sure who owns this 10/- me or your mother," but as a true friend he never said no. I never knew why Trevor's poverty was as bad as mine because his dad worked very hard, up at three every morning to go to the market. Maybe his pay was poor. My mom always paid him back his 10/- on Friday evenings without fail. My dad got paid on a Friday so some Fridays I was told to go and meet Dad outside his works at 1.00pm dinner time. He would come out and give me a 10/- note and 2d for my bus fare back home, he moaned every time, his cuss words were "Gad blimey".

When I got home, my mom would send me to the shops up the road to buy some food items, I was fit in those days I can tell you. Thinking about it if I got ten shillings the night before from Fred why did I sometimes meet my dad outside his works on a Friday dinner time to get money off him? Maybe Fred never got paid if his boss didn't go into work that Thursday. I do remember one Thursday I asked if Mom could borrow 10/- and he told me "tell your mom I haven't been paid today." It must have been on occasions like that when I had to meet my dad at his works.

78. THURSDAY PICTURES

Trevor's mom and my mom went to the pictures most Thursday evenings, the cinema was called the Atlas. It was the only couple of hours our moms had on their own, their bit of quality time without kids around them. One Thursday afternoon I had the bright idea to scrub the kitchen floor, they were red quarry tiles, I thought when she sees what I have done she will be delighted and take me to the pictures with her. I filled a bucket half full of water and threw the water onto the floor, flooding the kitchen, and got scrubbing with a big green bar of fairy soap and a worn-out scrubbing brush. After I had scrubbed half the floor, right I thought now I will tell Mom what I am doing and pictures here I come. I went round the house shouting, "Mom, Mom!" My sister Doreen said, "Mom's gone to the pictures with Trevor's mom." What a shock that was, I was horrified – she had slipped out of the front door and never closed it so I wouldn't know she had gone. I left the kitchen floor swimming in water and ran over the road to see Trevor.

"Trev, Trev," I shouted, "they've gone to the pictures without us knowing, let's run down Audley Road we might get there before they do." We ran non-stop till we reached the picture house and watched two buses go by. "We've missed them, Trev," I said, "that kitchen floor I left it swimming in water, my sister will go mad at me."

"Well don't go back in till later," he said. So I stayed out for a couple of hours then I thought I had better go and clean up that mess I left in the kitchen or I will get a good hiding from my mom. When I walked in, to my delight, Doreen had cleaned up my mess but she was hopping mad. "I had to clean all that water up you left!" she was screaming at me. I never made that mistake again. I left scrubbing floors to my mom, she used to scrub that floor on her hands and knees and then put newspaper down, we had to jump from one page to another, we dare not step on

190

the floor. The paper was left down until the floor was dry and by this time the paper was all dirty and ripped with us kids running in with our dirty pumps on. If she had enough pennies in the gas metre, she would light the oven to dry the floor quicker but that didn't happen too often, as she said with 3d (three pennies) she could feed her children so the floor could dry on its own.

79. COACH TRIP

Trevor came to me one day with what I thought was a brilliant idea. He had seen an advert in our local post office and Bowens the coach company were doing coach trips to a place called Leamington Spa. The whole town was lit up on the advert and it said 'Leamington lights'.

"Shall we go there, Dave?" Trevor said.

"Where is it, Trev?" I asked.

"I don't know, Dave, it sounds good though doesn't it."

"Yeah," I replied.

So off we went to Bowens to see how much it cost. I think it was 3/6 for children (three shillings and six pence 42 pennies).

"Right, Trev, we will have to run lots of errands to get the 7/- (seven shillings 84 pennies) we need."

"And we will need some spending money, Dave, we had better start right away," said Trevor.

"Yeah okay, Trev," I replied.

We worked really hard. We went back to knocking on doors for old rags and pop bottles, we fetched coal for our moms and neighbours, quarter hundred weight at a time (we never charged our moms), we made two shillings 2/- (24 pennies) fetching coal. We got up early to fit in all the errands we had agreed to do the day before, we worked hard for two weeks but we did it. We only had a 1/- (one shilling 12 pennies) each to spend that included our 3d (three pennies) bus fare to get back home.

The coach company wasn't far from our houses, only about a mile and a half maybe a little more, so we walked there. It only took twenty minutes or so to walk and that way we saved 3d bus fare. As we walked into the office a very pretty young lady greeted us, I was staring at her she was so pretty, I'm the same now anything that looks beautiful to me

I stare at no matter what it is. Suddenly Trevor gave me a nudge and said, "She's talking to you."

"Sorry, lady," I said, "but you are the prettiest lady I have ever seen." With a big smile she thanked me,

"Now, boys, how can I help you?"

"Can we book a coach please to see the lights, at um… where is it, Trev?"

"I can't remember, Dave."

"It must be Leamington lights you mean, boys."

We both said, "Yeah that's it, lady."

With a big smile she said, "You can't book a coach young man but you can book a seat."

"Yeah, that's what I meant lady, a seat. We want to sit together, we always sit together."

With a giggle she replied, "Yes, I think you wouldn't be very welcome sitting with the ladies." I hadn't a clue what she meant so we paid her the money and we got our tickets – we were very excited. Do you think she should have asked if we were allowed to go by ourselves?

We got the coach at 7.00pm, I remember that but for the life of me I can't remember where it picked us up from, neither can Trevor. You know not once did anyone ask "where are your parents?" or "who are you with?" I have a good memory but those lights are not very clear in my mind. It was a warmish night I remember, good job because our pumps had holes in the bottom but the cardboard was still intact. Both Trevor and me only had on jumpers (yes the same jumpers we got out of the sack of rags) at that time we did not possess coats. My mom bought all my clothes from the jumble sales and so did Trevor's mom. We weren't the cleanest two little boys in the city but no one passed any comments.

I do remember looking for a fish and chip shop and after what seemed a long time we found one, after all that walking we were hungry and thirsty. The chips we bought were 4d (four pennies) a packet. I was very surprised to see the chips, as they were crinkle chips, I had never seen crinkled chips before. The chips seemed to be hollow inside, I did not like them at all but I ate them because by this time we were both starving. We had bought a bottle of pop and shared it and the chips.

So back on the coach and to our surprise we were dropped off in the middle of Birmingham city centre, it was absolutely deserted, I had never seen it like it before and it was like a ghost town. We had no idea it would be so late when we got back, as young boys the time never entered our heads, we were just excited to be on our first coach trip. The one thing we had never thought about because we didn't know we were going to be dropped off in the middle of town is that after midnight the bus fares doubled and we had only saved 3d for our bus fare home. We tried to tell the bus conductor a sad story but he would not have any of it. "Please, Mister," I said, "it's a long way home and I only have 3d." He replied, "I told you 'No', clear off." He rang the bell and off the bus went with not one passenger on it, we were left standing there. I hope his son got better treatment from people than he gave to us.

So, we had about a ten-mile walk. It was creepy, there was not a soul to be seen anywhere. We got to the fire station in Gosta Green and it was getting quite chilly at this time, I started to shiver as we were both still in short trousers and no coats. As we passed the gun shop called Webley and Scott there were two police officers in the doorway, boy did they have a shock, because we were wearing pumps they didn't hear us coming. A policeman and a policewoman, such a scuffle, the lady police officer was attempting to pull down her skirt and the male officer adjusting his dress. He came from the doorway sounding very cross then he said, "What on earth are you young boys doing out at this time of night?" We explained we had not got enough bus fare to get home and that the conductor would not let us on the bus because after midnight the fares doubled, "So we are having to walk home."

"Does your mom know that you are out at this time of night?" "Yes," I replied. I really thought I was going to get a ride in a police car and be taken home, well I was hoping. With a wave of his hand he said, "Hurry up and get home, it's getting late." After saying that he went straight back into the doorway, I had not got a clue what they were doing.

My mom had no idea what time I got in, she was never worried about me at all. Trevor's mom and my mom let us do just what we wanted to do so long as we were out from under their feet (my mom's saying was 'go out get from under my feet'). Well they never knew what we had done, where we had been or that we had walked home from town at midnight. I asked Trevor if his mom knew what time he got in. He said she never missed him.

I wonder if you would you let your children do all the things we did?

80. HELPING BROTHER

My eldest brother Donald was in the R.E.M.E. as a regular soldier, he was sent to Korea to fight, he was there eighteen months and when he returned he was very ill suffering with T.B and Pleurisy. After coming out of hospital he had to find ways of making extra money because this wonderful country of ours don't look after their soldiers once they have done their bit for their country. So he started looking for scrap metal, in those days people used to dump their old cars on any piece of waste ground. Donald used to take the radiators off those old cars because they were made of copper and brass.

At that time the National Assistant Board visited Donald and looked round his house at all he and his wife possessed which was a bed, a table and two chairs. The visitor told him he was comfortable and he offered 1/- (one shilling 12 pennies) a week extra on top of his sick pay, which was not even enough to pay his rent. Donald told him what to do with his shilling and ordered him out of his house, as he was too ill to throw him out physically. Thank you, England, that's where I come in. Donald said if I collected metal from the tip, he would pay me.

So there I was back at the tip again looking for metal, we spent some hours on that tip, talk about Mud Larks we were the Tip Rats. I had done very well out of that tip in times past. Donald gave me a magnet and said any metal that doesn't stick to it put in the sack, bring the sack to me and I will give you half a crown 2/6d (two shillings and six pence 30 pennies). So I called for Trevor, told him and he couldn't wait to get started. After taking the filled sack to Donald he said, "I will weigh it in tomorrow if I feel a little better, so I will pay you the next day." We were very disappointed to say the least, we had planned to go swimming with the money we thought he was going to pay us.

Each day we went to the tip, there was new rubbish arriving all the time. One day was very good, we filled our sack quite quickly so off we went to my brother's with the bag of tat. "Here you are, lads, three shillings for that bag of tat yesterday and half a crown for this sack today. Get me another sack full like this one you brought today and I will give you two shillings and sixpence for the next bag."

Trevor and me went swimming the next day, the money was burning a hole in our pockets, we only earned money so we could go swimming and to the pictures. The very next day we were back on the tip, we had filled one and a half sacks with tat (can you imagine the state our clothes were in we did give our moms a hard time) when a very rough looking man came over to us shouting and swearing. He took our sacks and said, "These are mine now, now clear off this is my patch!" We had never seen him before, he was rough and dirtier looking than we were. "It's our tat Mister, we worked hard for it," I said. He tried to kick me but he missed, he terrified us both.

"Trev, I'm not letting him steal our tat, I'm going to get it back when he goes down the side of the tip. I'm going to run over there and get our sacks back." As I was stronger than Trevor, I said, "I will grab our two sacks, you grab his sack." When the man went down the side of the tip, we ran over and grabbed our sacks, he heard us and tried to get back up from the side of the tip quickly but he kept sliding down. We were running as fast as we could, he was shouting after us, language I had never heard before. Needless to say, we never went back to that tip, for a couple of weeks anyway. But it doesn't mean we stopped earning money, no way, we came up with all sorts of ideas. We got five shillings for those three bags of tat off my brother.

Donald changed his tactics from tatting to selling door-to-door. He decided to go to a warehouse and buy various items that he thought would sell, things like American comics, toys, combs and little boy dolls about two inches tall with a rubber dunce's hat on (which when filled with water and squeezed would wee). Donald asked me and Trevor if we would go door-to-door to sell these items for him, we were excited at the thought of earning extra money.

We sold three comics for a shilling, I remember one of the comics was called *Little Sheriff*. Pink, green and blue plastic combs, three for a shilling, I sold dozens of those. I was becoming a proper little salesman and so was Trevor. When I was asked where I got them from I said the same thing every time, "I'm selling them for my brother he's just come back from Korea, he's been fighting in the army he is very ill with T.B and Pleurisy." This was the truth, he was very sick for a very long time and I liked helping him and every shilling I made he gave me 2d (two pennies) for helping him, people were very kind when it was for a forces man.

When he got fed up selling those items from the warehouse, he started to get old cars to cut up and tat in. I must say that selling door-to-door taught me how to deal with the public. I became a salesman not long after I left school and so did Trevor, he became a sort of a car dealer, he lived his life around cars and did very well out of them.

81. THE BOYS' BRIGADE

I joined the Boys' Brigade and it was an organisation that I loved being part of. We always met up one evening a week and we had a football team, at that time in my life all I lived for was football and earning money of course, so I joined their team. I was asked what position I played, when I said in goal they were overjoyed. When I played in our first game, I realised why they were happy to have someone who had a little football skill, they were absolutely useless. We lost every match we played. I saved dozens of what would have seemed cert goals but we always lost, never less than (if my memory serves me right) sixteen nil, normally it was twenty or more. As they thought I was good they made me captain. I'm sure if there was a cup for the worst team in England's history, we would have won it, well we were in the papers as the team that likes losing twenty-nil on a regular basis.

I remember one game very well. We were twenty-two to nil down, I got so fed up I came out of my goal and dribbled the ball, past them all. I got to the goalie, he hadn't touched the ball all through the match, he must have been stiff and cold from having nothing to do. I scored, so we lost twenty-two to one. I bet that goalie hated me, the only time he had to make a save he missed, it was more luck than skill on my part. All part of growing up and I really enjoyed being part of the team even though we lost every game.

This Boys' Brigade met in the Lea Village area of Birmingham in a school known as Ridpool Road School. I only had part of the uniform, I was the only one that wore pumps as I didn't have any shoes, no one ever said anything I'm glad to say. I would have loved to have worn the same as everyone else but that wasn't to be. However, I was very happy to be there, they were good times.

82. SCOUTS

Being in the Scouts was also a happy time for me. At the top of my road, across the main road, was Audley Road and to the right was St. Andrews Church where the Boy Scouts held their meetings once a week. I tried to join several times but was always told there was a waiting list of two years.

One evening as I was passing the church, I noticed the Scouts were outside recognising different birds and naming them, well I thought I would try my luck, so I went up to the leader and asked him if I could join.

"You've tried before, haven't you?" he said.

"Many times," I replied.

"Okay," he said to my delight, "fill in this form and I will enrol you. Would you like to stay and join in the activities this evening?"

"Yes please," I replied.

"Right, sit in with that group sitting on the floor, they are being taught how to tie knots."

I was over the moon with excitement.

"Thank you very much," I said, I was so happy. He shook my hand and said, "Welcome to the Scout movement."

I told Trevor but he didn't want to join, so I tried very hard to get some money together to buy part of the uniform. I knew my mom could not afford to spend on items that were not essential, Mom's budget was small to say the least. I ran errands with Trevor and when I had earned three shillings I went to the Scouts shop in Birmingham city centre and bought a woggle, the next week I bought the neckerchief. I never did get any other parts of the uniform, a cap or jumper, at that time I was the only one that hadn't got a full uniform.

I was asked by one of the boys a few times, "How did you get to join? My friend has been waiting nearly two years to get into our group." In the end I told him a little white lie, I said I had been waiting over two years to join. I really loved being part of that group. We sometimes went to some woods called Yorkswood on the border of Shard End, sadly now a housing estate, we used to have paper chases, wild animal recognition and tree recognition. I loved all that, I was useless at it, but I enjoyed it. They held jamborees there, how often I'm not sure. We marched to church the last Sunday in the month as all those kinds of groups did in those days. We were expected to visit church every Sunday and were asked why not if we didn't attend. I loved to march with the band playing, I felt proud to be part of it all, to see the Sea Cadets, the Girl Guides, the Brownies, the Cubs and the Scouts all marching together was for me a wonderful sight.

I was part of that Scout movement for fifteen months or so. It would be nice to see the children marching these days and belonging to a group of one sort or another, of course in those days most of us didn't have a TV and computers were non-existent. After I left the Scout movement, I joined the Sea Cadets. Trevor never did join any of these groups with me, he joined the TA Army in Saltley.

83. THE SEA CADETS

In the same year I left the Scouts I joined the Sea Cadets. There on the parade ground, all in groups of about thirty, there must have been about one hundred and fifty Cadets. I only stuck it for four weeks, they didn't seem to do much, I never got any part of the uniform plus it just didn't appeal to me. I thought we would be sailing on the reservoir but that seemed rare, so I packed up that group.

I joined the Baptist Church confessed all my sins and became a Born-Again Christian. I loved all the people that were part of the Baptist movement, even the girls talked to me which was a shock. Girls normally looked down their noses at me but not those girls they were wonderful. That's the only time in my life that girls treated me nicely, mind you it never stopped me hating girls, well till I got older. I erm quite like the opposite sex now!

I must add when confessing my sins, the Preacher was surprised I hadn't sinned at all apart from scrumping apples. I still believe in Our Lord, but I do not attend church anymore.

84. TWO BLACK POODLES

I was sitting on my front garden wall one fine sunny morning wondering what I could do that day to earn some money so I could go swimming. While I was deep in thought, remembering I ran errands yesterday for Mrs Rowley so she wouldn't want any errands today, I suddenly nearly left my skin. Trevor had crept around the back of me and shouted down my ear, boy that broke my train of thought. He said, "Come on, Dave, let's go to town."

"I've no money, Trevor," I replied.

"It's okay, I will pay your fare, my dad just gave me some money."

So on the bus we went, through Stechford then the Pelham, Alum Rock, Saltley, Nechells, Gosta Green then town. It took about thirty-five minutes and we got off at the terminus called the Old Square. We walked to St. Martin's church, where there was a barrow boy and Trevor bought some damsons off him 3d (three pence) a bag but when we opened the bag to eat the damsons, they were all rotten. We went back and complained, the words he used I can't repeat! They went straight into the bin, 3d to us meant a lot, I could never treat children the way me and Trevor were treated.

We went to the rag market, it was packed. As we were walking round, we passed a stall where they sold crockery called Lees where I spotted in a box two black Poodles, in the begging position with glass eyes. They looked beautiful, they were made of chalk and they were 1/11d (one and eleven pence 23 pennies) for the two. I asked the man if he would save them for me till next week and he said, "Yes." But I didn't think he would for one minute.

"Can you make them any cheaper?" I asked him, I will leave his reply to your imagination.

Trevor asked, "What do yo want them for, Dave?"

I answered him with, "Well, Trev, we were selling all those things for my brother if yo remember, I thought we could go all round the houses and raffle them." Trevor's reply was, "Cor, Dave, what a brilliant idea."

So all the next week we ran errands and saved all the money we had earned, we didn't even go swimming. Come Saturday morning we went early to town, we thought the poodles were so good someone might buy them (well we were only children). Trevor said, "Don't ask him for them cheaper, Dave, he might not sell them to us." "Trev, after what he said to me last Saturday, I don't think I will." I bought the dogs. "Right, Trev, we need a raffle ticket book now," I said. We found one on a stall for 3d (three pennies), when we got back home (about one o'clock) we started in Trevor's road and we went down one side back up the other selling the tickets for 6d (sixpence) each. Trevor was holding the poodles up so they could see them.

We were known to most people because we had sold them comics, dolls, combs or toys. I did all the talking and when I was asked who gave you permission to sell door-to-door, I told a little white lie, I said they were being raffled for my brother who was very ill because he had been fighting in the army in Korea and now was in hospital. That was the truth about my brother (well apart from the hospital), I had told that story before when selling items for my brother, but the raffle that was for me and Trevor of course. They were happy to buy tickets because they thought they were helping an injured soldier who had been fighting for his country.

Well, we were threatened with the police, told to bugger off, called scruffy little urchins, and one or two other things I can't repeat. The one that stayed in my mind was a woman who threw her arms in the air, went hysterical and shouted, "Get away, get away! Those are made of chalk, it's unlucky, get away from my house!" and slammed the door in our faces. We sold two pounds five shillings worth of tickets then stopped selling. People did ask how would they know who had won, I told them we would go all around and tell everyone. They all put their names and addresses on the stub of the tickets, we did intend to go round but never did. We got a little lazy when the money was in our pockets.

Earning our pocket money "Buy a raffle ticket, Lady?"

We sat in my mom's kitchen and I said, "Who shall we give them to, Trev, shall we give them to Mrs Grayly she is as poor as we are?"

Trevor answered, "Yeah, Dave." So off we went. She only lived at the top of my road, we knocked on the door, her son opened the door and in a very stern voice he said, "Yes?" I jumped back with fear running all through my body, I told him, "You have won the raffle." His face lit up, "Mother, Mother!" he shouted, "we've won the raffle, thanks boys." As I walked away, I felt good inside, we had made someone happy. People were stopping us for a week afterwards asking who had won and why did you not come and tell us? We said we did but no one was in. We could have kept those dogs and no one would have known, well we would have known. We were very honest young boys keeping them never entered our heads.

85. LEAGUE CHAMPIONS

In my junior school I played football and at that time it was my life, I played centre forward. Well, 1955 was a magic year for me when we won the League Championship. My teacher Mr Lyceheart coached me, I liked him, he was very good to me. I enjoyed my time in juniors I was sorry to leave and go into the seniors.

While in the juniors I also used to do high jumping, I was high jump champion all through my school days, juniors and seniors, because I had a good spring in my legs. The teacher, Mr Green, who I didn't like very much, was my sports teacher. When I was doing my school work, he used to hit me across the back of the head, pick me up out of my chair by my

This photograph was taken when I was in the Juniors football team.
I am back row, second in from the right, 1955 was a special year for me.
Mr Lyceheart, the teacher.

hair and sometimes by my ear, that was the worst, by my ear. I was hopeless at my schoolwork and I was punished for it. I left school not being able to spell or read very well, but in sports I was okay, I could hold my own.

Mr Green thought he would try me in goal and I soon found out that was the position for me, I loved playing in goal. We never won a trophy

The one thing I was good at was high jumping.
I was school champion all through my school days.

Me, second from right in back row, wearing my football shirt, having had my photo taken five minutes before with the football team and told to leave the shirt on for this photo. This photograph was taken when I was in the Juniors in 1955.

but it was great to play football. Mr Green praised my sporting abilities but slapped me about when it came to my schoolwork. To be stood up in the school hall when in assembly and praised by the Headmaster for my achievements in sport for the school, if I'm honest it gave me a big head at times. Well, to be told how useless you are nearly every day it makes you feel good when told you are the best the school has when it comes to sport. When told things like this at times it can give a child a big head.

86. BULLYING

I was born with a perforated ear drum and I suffered with itchy ears all the time. I had to attend the school clinic once a week but I was accused by the Headmaster of crying wolf. I was a small boy needing treatment and refused treatment because grown-ups thought they knew best, but not this time. When my ear started running, I was taken to the Headmaster's office to show him, "Please, Sir, may I go to the clinic for treatment?" I was waiting for a slap across the head or the cane and to my surprise he looked and said, "So, you weren't crying wolf after all? Okay, you can go." He wrote out a note then handed it to me, "here is a note for the clinic."

So off I went, feeling very good because I was getting off school. As I walked into the clinic, boy those nurses were rougher than the teachers, I was ordered about just as though I had been naughty. I never was as a child I was always afraid of being punished, well I was punished by my teachers all the time because I was stupid (as I was always being told). I just couldn't remember anything I was taught the day before so I was pushed, poked, shook and slapped daily. The nurses had taken lessons from the teachers I reckon. Before I went in to see the doctor, they shouted to me to sit in the chair, not knowing which chair I was frogmarched and pushed (well, thrown) into the chair. When the nurse started poking my ear, she couldn't have been any rougher if she had used a shovel, the pain was making me cry. "Shut up, you baby," she said, it felt like she had cut my ear off and the blood ran down my face. She thrust a tissue into my hand, "Here hold that to your ear, now go and see the doctor," she growled.

As I walked in a very surprised look came over the doctor's face. "And what have you been up to, young man?"

"That nurse did it," I said.

"Oh," that's all he said.

After he stopped the bleeding, drops were put in my ear and a wad of cotton wool pushed hard into my ear, even that was giving me pain. Nothing else was ever done, it was for me to suffer, and children just did not count in those days. It was at that clinic that I found I had been born with a perforated eardrum and to this day still it troubles me. As I walked out of the doctor's room, I passed a nurse ordering some other poor boy about. I never did get a sorry or an apology, nothing, just a "Go on hurry back to school."

Back in school I went straight to my classroom and was greeted with, "Where have you been?" a slap on the back of my head and ordered to sit down. With my ear giving me pain, now the back of my head had pain, with cotton wool in my ear my hearing was only functioning at about 60 percent. Trying to do my writing I didn't hear the teacher shouting at me to pay attention, next thing was the blackboard rubber came flying across the classroom. Just at that moment I looked up, because by this time the teacher was screaming at me, to see what all the noise was about and the blackboard rubber glanced off my left eyebrow, right next to my eye a quarter of an inch nearer it would have damaged my eye. So now I had a bad ear, a headache and a lump on my left eyebrow.

I was ordered to pay attention and to bring back the blackboard rubber to the teacher. On doing this I was slapped again on the back of my head, ordered to go and sit down and pay attention in the future. I wonder if I met that teacher now, I'm 65 (at the time of writing) slapped him on the back of his head, grabbed him by his lapels and shook him violently there wouldn't be any difference would there? He slapped me about when I was defenceless, at his age now I would get locked up if I knocked him about, which he should have been for knocking about a defenceless child. I really would like to meet him to tell him what a rotten teacher he was. I was so afraid of him, I just couldn't concentrate on my school work which meant I learnt nothing. In turn this led to being slapped across the back of my head for not knowing how to do any lessons he even punched me in the stomach so hard I couldn't get my breath. I left school not knowing the difference between a signature and initials.

87. DOWN AND OUT

It was one Saturday morning I saw my mate John walking down the path to my house, I was coming back from the shops having done some shopping for my mom. With a very loud voice I shouted to him, "I've been looking for yo!"

He said, "Guess what? Na, don't think I should tell yo."

"Go on, go on, John, what is it?" I said, "Tell me, tell me."

"I have joined the Morris Commercial boxing club," he replied. "Yo ain't?" I questioned.

"I have honest," he replied, "I went with a boy from my school who was already a member of the boxing club." John was a Catholic and I'm Church of England so we both attended different schools. I hadn't seen John the evening before that's why I disbelieved him, he always told me everything he did so I was very surprised when he told me.

"Honest, Dave, I asked the trainer if he would let yo join," said John.

"Bet he said no," I replied.

"Well," said John, with a sad looking face and looking down at the floor, in a soft voice he said, "I was told to bring yo along Tuesday evening."

Well, I was so excited I jumped up and down and shouted, "Yeah, yeah!"

John said, "I thought yo would be pleased."

"Oh thanks, John, for asking for me, I'll start training right away," I said with great excitement. So we started to run what we called 'round the square' that was up my road, along Audley Road, past the row of ten shops then down Swancote Road till we reached my road and repeated it many times over. We were shadow boxing all the time we were running, boy did I have some grand ideas! About the third time around I was going to be world champion, I'm fit and strong, I was telling myself.

After we had stopped running, I was by my garden gate still shadow boxing, I must have looked a right idiot. Trevor came over to me, "What are yo doing?" he asked.

"I'm training, Trev," I answered.

"What for, Dave?" questioned Trevor.

"I'm going to be a boxer," the whole time I was talking to him I was shadow boxing, "John has joined the boxing club down Alum Rock and he has got me in, I will ask for yo Trev," I told him.

"Na, I don't want to box, our Tony went there some time ago," Trevor said. So, I went with Trevor to talk with his brother Tony, he said he liked it but just stopped going, "Try it, Dave, you will like it," he said.

So come Tuesday evening, I think that was the night or it might have been Thursday evening, any road up I started at the boxing club. I was training with a medicine ball, after that we all did roadwork, that's running round the streets. I felt good, my ideas of becoming a champion grew even stronger. I did all this for a few weeks and even did some sparring in the ring with older boys. I held my own, mind you they weren't hitting to hurt, only getting me used to the feel of the ring.

After a few months I had my first bout when a visiting team came, it was only a friendly so we could gain more experience, three rounds lasting three minutes. My turn came and out I came for the first round, I was quicker than my opponent, I jabbed with my left, I only threw my right once, I remember he never laid a glove on me. Yeah, I thought, this is easy, I am going to win this fight, end of round one. The trainer was well pleased with me, he said, "Just keep doing what you are doing, it's in the bag." Round two, out I went, really cocky if I'm honest, my opponent came out, hit me with a left hook and knocked me out with one punch, I'm ashamed to say. I was out for nearly three hours, not knocked out completely but not able to stand on my own two feet for quite a while, that day was the end of my boxing career. Some champion, eh?

101… 102… 103… I don't think he wants to play anymore.

88. OUR PARK

Glebe Farm Park is in Stechford and I spent many hours in that park. The River Cole runs through the park and on the edge of the park there is an alleyway that runs the whole of the length of it. The front cover of my book *Pumps with Holes in* is loosely based on that alleyway, at one end of it there is a road called Colehall Lane and at the other end is Bushberry Road. Halfway up the pathway was a very big tree, probably an oak tree, and we used to have rope tied to the tree and swing across the river. Most of the boys that lived around Glebe Farm and Shard End used to play by the river.

One dry day we were playing on the swing, my friend Trevor and me, when a bully boy came up to us and told us to get of the swing as he was now going to use it. He wasn't a school boy, I reckon he was in his twenties. Me and Trevor weren't bullies at our young age, well at any age, I suppose you could call us cowards, well to be very honest at that time in our lives we were cowards, yes for sure we were. The bully got hold of the rope, ran in a circle and went sailing through the air shouting, "Yeah, yeah, this is great I haven't done this in a long time!" He was very well dressed, he had on what looked like a new suit, but in those days everyone seemed well dressed to Trevor and me. He went across the river twice, on the third time as he was coming back across the river, the rope snapped. The river was quite deep at that time and he disappeared under the water, which looked very dirty. We stood on the bank laughing and shouting abuse at him, only because we felt safe where we were and knew he wouldn't be in the mood to chase us, well I did say we were cowards. We shouted as we were running away, "We are glad yo went into the cut!"

Trevor said, "Ay, Dave, I hope we don't bump into him again."

"Cor Trev and I do, I'm staying away for a while, Trev," I said.

215

"Yeah, me too, Dave," Trevor agreed.

We never did see him again that bully boy.

A long time after that we went back to the tree to play swinging across the river, this time we were with our other friends Billy, Johnny, Eddy, but Dougie wasn't with us that day. As we approached the big tree, there were lots of lads from our school playing on it and just as one boy went to swing across the river the rope snapped. Fortunately, he didn't go into the river, he clung to the side of the river bank to save himself from falling in and he shouted, "Has anybody got a decent rope?"

Billy shouted back, "Yes I've got a rope, it's a great big thick one, it's that thick it will carry ten men but I want it back when you've finished with it."

They all shouted, "Go on, Bill, get it now."

Billy asked me if I'd go home with him to get the rope as he needed help to carry it, he told me it was his dad's rope, it was a black tar rope and very thick. "Wow!" all the boys gasped when they saw the rope that would hold ten men. Up the tree Billy went, it took a while before he caught the rope, so by this time there were about sixteen lads all wanting to be first. Alan Blackwell's brother (whose name I can't recall) won first go by picking the shortest straw. He took a good run and swung across the river, when the rope snapped on his way back and into the river he fell, he scrambled out dripping wet. All he said as he walked off home was, "Ten men!" He disappeared across the park, he didn't have very far to walk as his house and garden backed onto the park.

I was pushed into the river at that same spot many times over the years, we never learn, well I didn't that's for sure. I also went to collect grass with a boy named Reg. I never played with him and was surprised one day when he asked me to help him pick grass for his rabbits. Near the river where the swing used to be there were spiked railings, inside there was long lush green grass, so we climbed over the railings and picked quite a big bagful. Reg suddenly threw the bag over the fence and shouted, "Dave, come on quick, get over the railings!" I became very frightened seeing the look on his face and his hurried actions. I got over those railings much quicker than when I went in, I can tell you. Reg ran much faster than me, he was about three years older and when we reached the road puffing, panting with our lungs screaming for air, I finally got my words out and asked him what the matter was. What he told me worried me for a long time afterwards, he said there was a man creeping up on us on his belly. It took me a long time to go back to that place again.

When we played on those rope swings, they of course got worn out very quickly and eventually would break. We never knew where all those ropes came from but I will always remember that thick black tar rope of Billy's the most. To this day it brings a smile to my face whenever I think about it.

89. CYCLING

We went to Kenilworth Castle many times on our bikes, but one occasion stands out in my mind far more than any other. It was a warm sunny morning and I was sitting on my front garden gate when Johnny came down the road from the shops, he had run an errand for someone. He shouted very loudly, "Hi Pross!" He was always very loud, one of those boys you could hear and pick out in a crowd and know exactly where he was, but he was a great mate of mine. He asked, "What yo doing today?"

"Nunk," I answered, I always used that common word 'nunk', meaning of course 'nothing'. Thinking about it, all or nearly all my speech was in common Brummie slang, I had quite forgotten about it. Words such as nunk, nowt, spondulucks, akers, 2/6 two and a kick, 2/6d half a dolla, 5/- a dolla, 10/- ten shillings half a bar, 10/- ten shillings half a sheet, £1 a sheet, £1 a wonna, 6d a tanner, 1/- a bob ain't, wunt, gob, bin, yow and sharnt. Us boys had our own language and many more slang words like 'bin' means 'been' and 'gooin' means 'going', I think I would need another lifetime to write them all down, well another book anyway. Thinking about it I did write another book with the way we talked it's called *Just a Brummie*.

"I thought we could go to Kenilworth Castle," Johnny said.

"I'm game," I said, so off we went to call on our other mates Trevor, Billy and Eddy. Dougie had stopped going around with us, I think he had to make sure the pigs were all right. We all agreed and we set off half an hour later. None of us had any money, food or water to take with us we never did, we lived like that all the time. We looked after each other and we did whatever we could to survive.

From Glebe Farm to Kenilworth Castle seemed a very long way, I drive it now in the car and I always say the same thing, how on earth as young lads on bikes with no food or water did we do a long run like this? We did it many times.

I remember going across Stonebridge Island on the way to Kenilworth, it was just a country lane then, now it's a major road. All riding together, if we saw blackberries we would pick some as well as damsons, apples, swedes and carrots from the farmer's field. We only took what we could eat, no more, never destroyed anything and of course it depended on the time of year what we ate. It usually took us about an hour and a half to two hours to reach the Castle depending on how many stops we made.

The Castle was wrapped up in scaffolding, we walked with our bikes around the outside and picked a spot where we could climb over the wall, well we couldn't pay to go in as none of us had a penny to our name. The first place we headed for was the water tap, thinking back now I can't remember where it was situated, what I do remember was the ones waiting for a drink would be saying to whoever was drinking, "Come on, hurry up

My friends and I at Kenilworth Castle.

we all want a drink!" When we were all watered (I would like to say and fed but alas water was all we had), we would climb and investigate the ruins.

Billy who was skinny, wiry and also very daring, decided to climb to the top of the scaffolding, he got right to the top. Then Billy suddenly appeared staggering from the back of the castle, he looked in a very bad state. It turned out he had slipped off the top scaffold bar and hit every bar on the way down, those bars being rough because of the concrete that was on them were like rubbing sandpaper on one's skin. Every bar he hit took skin off some part of his body and he must have hit the ground with a thud. It took five minutes for him to properly come around. What a state. Fortunately, he hadn't any broken bones, so we all climbed back over the wall where we had left our bikes and walked back to the road. By now Billy had recovered some of his senses but was badly bruised, battered, skinless and very sore. He was just about to get on his bike when two cyclists stopped, the lady asked, "What happened to you?" We told her, she was very sympathetic and took out her first aid kit and cleaned him up, she was very thoughtful, what kindness she showed. We returned to Kenilworth Castle a few times after that, but none of us ever climbed on any scaffolding again especially not Billy.

90. PAPER BOY

When I was thirteen years old, I got a paper round that paid 13 shillings a week. So I went to Hunts Radio Shop where they also sold bikes and records and my mom signed for me to buy a bike on H.P. (hire purchase) and I paid for it out of my paper round money. It was a Raleigh bicycle.

At that time I adored a girl named Carol who was in my school, I suppose it was puppy love at the age of thirteen, she lived in the road opposite the paper shop that I delivered papers for. On the way home from school we took a short cut through an alleyway which ran through a field known as the home guard field. It was in this field I had my first kiss and cuddle, it was very passionate or so it seemed at that time. The next day at school I plucked up the courage to ask her to be my girlfriend and go out with me, she smiled and said, "Yes." All my nerves jumped, I was so excited, nothing in my young life had made me feel like I did the moment she said yes.

Every day I walked her to her road, she was adopted and her adopted father had forbade her to have anything to do with lads. After walking her to her road one day, as I was on my way to the paper shop, I stood talking to Carol at the top of her road when a gaze of total fear came into her eyes, "It's my dad," she said trembling. He was a little white-haired man, slightly bent forward in a raging temper. I was nervous, I just waited there to say hello to him, just to prove to him everything was okay because I knew how over-protective he was as Carol had previously told me. Just as I was about to say hello, without a word, his right hand came round and gave me one almighty slap around the face which hurt my ear. Instinctively I swung my right fist at him, fortunately I missed, but as he walked away slapping Carol round the head, in a hurt rage I shouted, "If you touch me again, I will kill you." I laugh when I think about it now, as a skinny thirteen year old I couldn't have slapped him, never mind killed him.

Next day at school I was summoned to the headmaster's office and told I must never talk to Carol again, it turned out her dad had been up to the school that morning and told the headmaster that under no circumstances must Carol talk to any boys. In a mixed school that was impossible especially as she was a rebel and her dad didn't know, it made the whole episode a joke, so I had been given a smack round the ear for nothing. The laughable thing about the situation is that on the day she said she would be my girlfriend on that very evening she also arranged to go out with someone else. I learned of this about a week later from a lad who was in the same class as me and also lived in my road. At the time I was really hurt seeing as she was my first real puppy love.

It turned out she loved the attention she got from boys and the boys were only too willing to pay her attention, the strange thing is she never ever told me she was going out with another boy. I never got angry about it and I talked to her every day even though I wasn't supposed to.

91. MORNING DEW

My friend Dougie had two girl cousins who he said were jolly and liked a good laugh, they lived in Polesworth in Staffordshire. I just couldn't wait to meet them, but for some reason and I can't remember why, we never did meet those girls. We all went there on our bikes to look round the place, it was very nice and on the way back we stopped at Tamworth where there was an open-air lido in the park, we all liked swimming in the open air.

Sometime later my other friend Johnny suggested that we go to Polesworth camping for a few nights. Johnny brought a loaf of bread and a block of butter. I got a jar of jam, a packet of tea and a bag of sugar just for the two of us. Johnny brought the primus stove, a saucepan and a frying pan but there was one little drawback, we hadn't got a tent! What I had was a threadbare towel and Johnny had a mac, nothing else, to say we were not prepared is an understatement. It was a very warm summer so we assumed it would be all right, we got on our bikes and off we went.

It was great fun cycling there. We went through Tamworth to get to Polesworth and we found a nice spot where some of the local lads swam. We were asked many times, "Do you come from Brum?" in those days they didn't see many Brummies. Polesworth was a beautiful little village, one boy asked, "Are you camping here?"

"Yes," we replied.

"Watch out for the farmer, he doesn't like people on his land, we always swim here in the basin, he catches us sometimes and gives us a clip round the ear," he then asked, "Where is your tent? You will be cold by the river."

"We will be okay, I'll light a fire," I replied.

"Don't forget about the farmer, if he catches you with a fire, you really will be for it. Is that all the food you have?" he asked.

"We've eaten half the loaf, we still have half the loaf left and butter we will be okay," we said to him.

"You can't survive on just that," he commented, then Johnny reminded me we had jam as well.

"That's still not enough, would you like me to bring you some eggs back later?" he shouted as he walked away, "I'll be back in about an hour."

"We have no money," I shouted to him.

"You don't need any, I know where they are free range, I know where the chickens lay them," he said.

About an hour and a half later he returned with four eggs, how wonderful to live in the countryside and get free food like that, one would never go hungry. We thanked him and said how kind he was, "I'll see you tomorrow," he said. "If you want any more eggs, I'll get them for you." He shouted "Bye!" as he crossed the field. We gathered up as much firewood as we could and got a real good fire going. Out came the frying pan, we melted the butter in the pan, I cooked two of the eggs and with two pieces of bread we made egg sandwiches. We felt really good, "this is the life ain't it Johnny? We will have to come camping again," I said.

"Yeah," replied Johnny, "this is great ain't it, Dave?"

"You know what Johnny, I'm going to live out doors when I grow up."

"Good idea, Dave. We could travel the world together." What a dream, well the thought was good or so we thought at that moment in time. I carefully placed the other two eggs in with the rest of the bread so they wouldn't get broken. "We'll have the other two eggs for breakfast," Johnny said, so we saved those two eggs even though we were still hungry.

We decided to have a swim in the river after we had eaten, we had a great time swimming with the local boys, they all were skinny dipping as they put it, I had never heard that saying before. Me and Johnny wore trunks. After swimming and drying ourselves on the towel it was so wet we lay it by the fire in the hope it would dry enough to put over us when night time came but it never dried. It was far too wet, so we tried to put

THE CAMPFIRE BURNING

A.WAITE

Enjoying the great outdoors without a tent.

the mac over both of us and the wet towel on top of the mac. Fire going, all seemed good at that moment in time and we fell asleep.

Then the worst of the nightmares started. I woke up shivering, wet and very cold, the fire had gone out, we didn't know mist from the river would soak everything. Trying to light the fire was almost impossible, everything was so wet, but we finally got the fire going again and as we got warm, we fell asleep. Early in the morning it was beautiful to see the white mist rising from the river and the sun shining through the trees. Johnny said, "I'm going in for a swim." I lit the camping stove and made two cups of tea with water from the river, as the water boiled the scum that came to the top of the water looked like green slime with other colours mixed in with it, I never gave it a thought, I just scraped it out and made the tea. I drank my tea but Johnny left his to cool down. "I will cook those two eggs after I've had a swim," I said to Johnny. We were enjoying ourselves so much we didn't notice what was going on around us. Johnny suddenly said, "I'm hungry, I'll cook those two eggs, Dave."

"Okay, John," I said, "give me a shout when you've cooked them." As he climbed up the bank, he gave out an almighty shout, "Oh no Dave! Come and look at this, the cows have eaten all our food and trodden all over our cooking equipment."

I laughed. "Oh yeah," I said, "pull the other one."

"No, Dave, it's true. Come and have a look." To my surprise he was right, they had eaten all our food, they had trodden on the frying pan and ruined the primus stove, so we had no food or equipment. Johnny was so angry he threw everything into the river, the great outdoor explorers were beaten after only one night.

We cycled to Tamworth Park to the lido as it was another very warm day. We lay on the grass and dozed off for a short while as the sun shone on us and made us feel very comfortable, we woke up feeling very relaxed so we just lay there for about another thirty minutes or so reminiscing about our great outdoor adventure and agreed we would do it every year but with all the right equipment then we cycled home. My bed was such a wonderful and welcome sight, I slept like a log and next morning it was back to normal.

We never did go back of course, but if ever you go camping by a river don't be stupid like we were, take a tent. We never had any money so we made the best of what we had. I have all these wonderful memories of that one night's camping and many happy years growing up with my friends.

92. MY DAD

As I've already mentioned my dad worked at the Metropolitan Carriage and Wagon Works situated at Saltley in Birmingham. Every night when he walked in from work he smelled of suds, which was a liquid soap that was used to cool down the drills when going through thick metal that Dad was drilling. All his clothes became very shiny, his flat cap was that shiny I could have skated on it. He wore that same cap every day, it hung in the hallway with his waistcoat and overcoat, they were retired the same day as Dad retired.

When he was a working man, he drank very heavily. Before he went to bed, he would count all his cigarettes that were left in the packet and he would count all his change and put it in separate piles of copper and silver. He even counted the nubs in his waistcoat pocket that he hung in the hallway. No matter how drunk he was, he did this every time he took himself to bed.

I started to smoke at the age of thirteen (I stopped smoking when I was 38), I would take a nub out of his waistcoat pocket and, when he got up, he told me he knew I'd had a nub out of his pocket.

One Sunday afternoon he really was the worse for drink, more than he normally was, so he took himself to bed without having his dinner. I waited until he dropped off into a deep sleep then I woke him and asked him if I could have next week's pocket money, in our house we never got pocket money all the time. He said, "Take a shilling off the shelf," which was over the gas fire in the bedroom.

So, the next Saturday afternoon I thought I would try the same trick again. He was the worse for drink again but not as bad as the week before so I waited until I thought he'd got into a deep sleep, then I shook him and was shouting down his ear, "Dad, Dad, can I have my next week's pocket money this week and I won't have my pocket money for

227

next week?" To my surprise he jumped out of bed and said, "You think I'm stupid, you came that last week," he threw me out of the bedroom and said, "don't you ever wake me again when I'm asleep!" No matter how drunk he was, when it came to his money and cigarettes, he always knew exactly how much money he had and how many cigarettes.

93. PAWN SHOP

Once a week my mom took whatever she could to the pawn shop, sometimes she would get 2/6d (32 pennies), sometimes 1/6d (18 pennies) and sometimes only 6d (6 pennies). Once or twice when I took some items of clothing, they wouldn't give me anything on them. The pawn shop was on Wyndhurst Road in Stechford, by the Atlas picture house (my local flicks which has since been demolished). I hated going to that pawn shop, it smelt funny and it was dark and dismal.

My mom had to pawn her wedding ring one day, they gave her 10/6 (ten shillings and six pence – 126 pennies) on it, she told me that broke her heart and she never ever got it back. Many years later she bought herself a new wedding ring, my wife Irene got it for her out of her catalogue. If it wasn't for that pawn shop I would have gone hungry more than once, so I suppose I mustn't knock it too much, they even laid on a special bus to take people to that pawn shop. It was always called nunkies in our house, never the pawn shop, why nunkies I'm not sure although I believe pawn shops were known as 'uncles' maybe nunkies was said instead of uncle. It isn't there anymore but I'm sure people still could do with it.

As I was approaching the age of fourteen, I bought a lovely blue suit on the 'glad and sorry', I paid 1/6 every week (18 pennies) which I earned by running errands. My mom of course had to make believe she was buying it for me. It was the first suit I had ever owned and I only wore it on special occasions. As I didn't have a wardrobe in my bedroom, I had a picture rail running all around the bedroom about eighteen inches from the ceiling and I used to hang my suit with a coat hanger on the picture rail. I loved that suit.

One afternoon I went to put it on, for what occasion I can't remember, to meet a girl probably. Only to find it wasn't there. Mom hadn't been not very well off that month, she had pawned my suit two weeks before and, can you believe it, I hadn't missed it hanging on the wall and all that was in my bedroom was a bed. It's sad to say I never got that suit back, money was always very short in our house.

94. MOM'S CAKE STAND

Off our kitchen was a walk-in pantry and in there was a concrete slab over the gas meter called a cold slab, the purpose of this was to keep the meat and various foods cold as we didn't possess a fridge in those days, but then again not many people did. Well not where we lived anyway. On the right-hand wall was the electric meter and on the left-hand wall were three wooden shelves one above the other. On the top shelf was a glass with Mom's false teeth in there, they stayed there until they no longer fitted her because one's face alters with age, even though she hadn't worn them for over forty years she wouldn't throw them away.

On the other end of the top shelf was a cream cake stand that was purchased from Woolworths for 6d (six pennies) long before the day I was born. It was used rarely in our house except for Christmas Day when it was put on the table in the living room at teatime. Mom told me that when she bought that cake stand that all the items that Woolworths sold at that time cost 6d (six pennies). This cake stand was Mom's pride and joy, I remember her lending it out a couple of times to her friend Lizzie for birthday parties. It got chipped on the underside, which upset Mom quite a bit, none of us children were ever allowed to wash or carry that cake stand. I am very proud to say I now own that very cake stand.

I remember one afternoon after school had ended for the day I walked into the living and to my surprise the table was laid with fruit, sandwiches, jelly and Mom's wonderful cake stand was in the middle of the table with a cake on it. I was excited I can tell you, I hadn't a clue what was going on, there was not a soul to be seen, then in walked my sister Doreen with her fella or as Doreen put it "her chap", my mom and other people as well. It turned out Doreen had been up to Birmingham Register Office in the city centre and got herself married. I was glad she was married, it meant I was going to eat all those nice things on the table,

My mom on a rare day out.

it was a rare treat and a lovely surprise. Lenny, Doreen's husband, told me years later that Trevor's mom Lizzie had laid out the table for them, they didn't know she was going to do it, what a wonderful lady. Lenny has always been a great son-in-law and a great brother-in-law to me.

95. MY MOM'S DEAR FRIEND RITA HILL

A very close friend of my mom's was Rita Hill (who I've already mentioned) and I'm pleased to say still to this day a friend of mine and her sister Ann was a friend of my sister Janet. Rita lived in Swancote Road, just across the road from our house. Trevor lived next door to Rita at No 45. Rita was still at school at that time but when she was supposed to be there, she would sneak out of school and go to our house, walk in through the back kitchen and shout, "I've come to wash up for you, Pross!" She always called Mom 'Pross'. Mom loved Rita and always referred to her as "our Rita" like she was her daughter. As well as her sister, Ann, she also has a brother named Barry we all played together from time to time. Happy days, eh Rita, I'm glad you are still my friend.

96. SHOPS REMEMBERED

The first recollection I have of our fish and chip shop was paying 3d (three pennies) for a bag of chips, then 4d (4 pennies), then they went to 6d (six pennies) and they stayed that price for a very long time. I can still see in my mind's eye those fryers, they were in the style of the 1930s, Art Deco. There were mirrors on the back of the fryers which were situated against the back wall, opposite the counter where they served the customers and they had a chrome edge all around them, they looked like an opened fan. The outer mirrors were plain green, the middle mirror was green with a picture of an old sailing ship with sails on it, I remember it so well because I admired it so much, I used to stare at it and study the art, I just loved the shape of the whole fryer. The owner always asked if you had brought your own newspaper to wrap your fish and chips in. I've seen those chips put straight on to the newspaper, I'd even taken piles of newspaper to him myself, it never hurt us, in fact it was a pleasure to eat fish and chips straight out of the newspaper. I've eaten my share of newspaper ink. I wonder how many germs we ate from those old newspapers they never knew how clean the people were that gave them those newspapers.

Wrensons was the shop that is most vivid in my mind only because of the bacon slicer. That slicer used to fascinate me, the big wheel they turned to make the bed of the slicer move backwards and forwards. I stood and watched that machine doing its work while my mom was being served. The machine, to me, seemed to be dancing, I just loved that movement. On a white marble slab was a cheese cutter that was also fascinating to watch, a piece of wire with a wooden handle secured on the end of the wire was placed on top of a big block of cheese. The manager (whose name was Oakley) would say to whoever he was serving, "Is that too big or is it all right?" as he positioned the wire on top of the cheese. If it was okay he pushed down on the wire with no

235

effort at all and the wire cut though the cheese perfectly, he then wrapped it very neatly in greaseproof paper.

Presentation in those days showed pride. Slabs of butter were wrapped up in the same way as the cheese. When Mom bought 2oz of tea it was put in a blue cone shaped bag and the sugar was also weighed and put in a blue bag, they folded the bags very expertly so the contents would not fall out.

The front window of the shop was big with two handles at each side at the bottom so the window could be slid upwards. Behind the window was a large white marble slab with bacon laid on it in rows. In the summer when it was warm that window was opened, talk about health and safety, can you imagine all the dust and the flies landing on that bacon and who knows what else. Trouble was in those times there weren't any fridges, it's hard to imagine now. My mom told me that on one sunny day when she was passing that shop with my brother Kenny the window was open displaying bacon in neat rows and Kenny slapped every pile of bacon as he passed. This led to Mom having an argument with Mr Oakley, the manager, because he shouted at Mom to keep her kids in order. Mom replied, "I bring up children not kids, kids are young goats." I can imagine what Mr Oakley must have thought when Mom said that to him.

In our two rows of shops were Stockton the newsagent, Holidays the butchers, and next to the butchers was a children's clothes shop The Walkin which was originally a fancy goods shop. Then there was Braggs cake bread and cooked meats shop, Wrensons groceries, Tranters hairdressers, Wilkes a grocery shop, Goldings Chemist, the Post Office, Browns the greengrocers and then the Co-op butchers and Co-op Groceries. On the opposite side of the road were Lathems haberdashery, the butchers, Hunts radio and bicycle shop, Saxons men's clothes shop, Paynes shoe repairers, the fish and chip shop, Turners seed merchants, Carmichaels faggot and peas shop, Suches hardware shop and The Glebe public house.

Across the main road there were several more shops whose names do not come to mind apart from Ted Haynes, Stanley James, Vernons Gowns, Taberers newsagents, a shoe shop, a butchers and an outdoor (the parents of a boy from my school ran that shop).

97. DISRESPECTFUL CHILDREN

As I grew up with my three sisters there was a word I learned that was used very frequently in our house, I must admit if I could take it back I surely would, that word was "rotten".

As the girls came home from school at dinner time, when they walked into the kitchen, if they saw dinner was not to their liking they would say something like, "What's this rotten stuff?"

"I don't want it, I don't rotten like it."

"We had this rotten stuff last week."

"I told you I didn't like this rotten stuff last rotten time."

Mom would say, "Stop using that word 'rotten'."

Their reply would be, "Well you know I don't rotten like it."

As I got older, I automatically started to use it and it became normal speech in our house, going something like this, "What's for dinner, Mom, not rotten stew I hope?" We rarely had puddings in the week, I would ask after dinner, "Is there any pudding?" When I heard the word "yes" I got excited, "Corr, what is it, Mom?"

"Ball sago pudding," she would reply. I hated that rotten stuff and I still do! "Well bloody well go without then," she would say and I did. My sisters loved it, so I had to watch them eat it. I would be saying, "It's not rotten fair, they got rotten pudding." Mom would say, "Well serves you right, they have had your share." All I would say was, "It's not rotten fair, it's not rotten fair."

I think Mom got a little used to us talking like we did. But one time that really sticks in my mind I was in my teens, I think I was fourteen at the time. Mom must have had a bad day, I had been playing football in the horse road, Mom called me in for my tea it at 4.30pm. I remember as I walked in, I took one look at the dinner and said "Stew! I'm rotten fed up of rotten stew." Mom shouted at me saying, "And I'm rotten fed up of you saying rotten, now it's got to stop, if you say rotten one more time, I will put this bloody plate of dinner over your bloody head." I said, in a very cheeky manner, "Oh yeah," and Mom picked up the plate of stew and tipped it over my head, keeping her hand firmly pressing on the plate. The stew ran down the back of my head and down my neck, over my face and all down the front of my shirt. She looked me square in the eyes and with a fierce look on her face she said, "Well?" I was so shocked at what she had done I remember saying, "It's better on the plate, Mom."

"Let that be the last time you talk to me like that, you hear?"

"Yes, Mom, I'm sorry," I replied. I had to have a wash down as there were not enough pennies to put in the gas meter to heat the water for a bath. I also had to wash my shirt and dry it as it was the only shirt I possessed.

That was the last time, if my memory serves me right, I ever said that to my mom. My younger brother John told me he tried saying 'rotten' to Mom because he had heard me say it, he said she gave him such a smack round his ear and told him she would not allow it anymore so he never did again. I never did that's for sure. We were very cheeky to you Mom but every one of your children loved you very much.

98. MISDEMEANOURS

We used to fare dodge on the West Midlands buses and trains, we had worked out a plan. We would get on the bus and go downstairs, when the conductor came to collect the fare we would get up from our seats as though we were getting off and as the conductor was taking a fare, we would walk past him and he would take no notice of who was walking past him, so upstairs we would run. The conductor had to concentrate on giving the correct change as you did not have to have the correct fare to pay as you do nowadays. We never ever tried it when a lady conductor was on duty, they never seem to forget who's paid and who hasn't, men on the other hand didn't seem to be as dedicated.

Another thing I did was to put bus tickets from past journeys into my top pocket and then the dodge I used was to take the appropriate coloured ticket from my pocket, hold it in my hand with my face pressed up the window. Trevor would do the same, with the ticket in full view so as the conductor walked up the aisle shouting, "Any more fares please!" it looked like we were looking out of the window innocently with our hands on the sill, as he walked past it looked like we had paid. We did this many times, we were never caught, as we were looking out of the window, I would say things like, "That's the shop we went to," I could never think of anything else to say. Well, it worked every time, we always had enough money to pay the fare just in case we were caught out by the inspector we could never fool them.

Trevor and I used to chew lots of chewing gum. There was a machine on our Post Office wall that gave out a free packet every fourth turn of the knob. We tried many times to fiddle that machine by putting chewing gum on the back of the penny to make it stick so the penny would not go into the machine but it never worked. Every packet had four pieces of sugar-coated gum inside it, if we only had one penny between us, we would buy a packet and have two pieces each. We always shared and looked after each other, we never ever fell out that I can remember.

The Post Office also had a cigarette machine outside the shop and a milk machine which held what was then new cardboard cartons with a pint of milk inside them. In those days if a shop stayed open after five o'clock you were very lucky, that milk machine would have been a god send to people working late. When we put our sixpence in, we found if we kicked the front of the machine really hard, we got two cartons of milk instead of one, after a few months that machine was so damaged it was taken away. The cigarette machine suffered the same fate as the milk machine and was taken away.

In those days the phone boxes had A and B buttons, if you couldn't get through to whoever you were calling you pressed button B to have your money refunded. We found that by pushing a piece of rag up the return coin tray in the telephone box, when people would press button B to get their money back no coins would fall. They would be punching, kicking, shaking and also putting their fingers up the return compartment to see if the coins had got stuck, then eventually they would give up. After they had gone, we would go in with a piece of wire with a hook on the end, push it up the return slot, hook the rag, pull it down and out would come the coins. But I preferred to make my money by running errands for the neighbours, the rewards were more satisfying and of course, honest, which I preferred to be.

99. A BIG THANK YOU

Of course, in our lives each day we do things similar to the day before and this book only highlights some of the happenings in my life.

A big thank you to my mom whose love and devotion gave me the knowledge to overcome poverty and to show respect to rich and poor alike and to always have good manners. She had to bring up seven children with never enough money to clothe us properly, to feed us or keep us warm most of the time. She was always there for her children. Many, many times she gave us her last pennies as we came first in her life. She could make sixpence last for three days by buying bones from the butchers for the dog (which we hadn't got) with a pound of potatoes costing only a 1d (one penny), a pennyworth of carrots and with an onion she would boil it all up, she got us through the week. My dad was no help at all, well most of the time. She lived like this well into her fifties. Even after we got married she gave us love and attention and even lodgings too when houses were very hard to get.

Thank you Mom, we all love you very much.

Her children Donald, Kenneth, Kathleen, Doreen, Janet, David and John.

I wrote a poem for my brothers and sisters and I've included it on the next page.

100. TO MY BROTHERS AND SISTERS

An uncommon surname have we
Prosser, it is and will always be.
Common values, common link,
As a family a true bonded link.
Seven of us grew up together,
Brothers and sisters no one can sever.
As a family there is no better.
Each of us was born unique,
None the same.
But what we share is the Prosser name,
Please always remember this.
Our wonderful Mother Dora
Blessed us all with a loving kiss.
Written for you all with love.

Brother David Prosser, born 30th October 1943

101. A POEM BY THE AUTHOR

Down our street when I was young
We played games all day long.
Hide and seek, tip cat, Polly on the Mopstick,
Lots of games like that.
Football was my favourite game
I played this time and again.
I was poor but that didn't matter
When playing games I forgot the latter.
The only vehicles I used to see were horse-drawn carts,
No others I see.
So playing games in the street was not hard,
Nothing ever stopped me not even those carts.
Those open spaces I used to know
Were down my street where I still go.

102. BECOMING AN ADULT

In 1958 there were three terms for leaving school: Easter, Summer and Christmas. All my friends that I grew up with left in the Easter and Summer of 1958 and went to work. I didn't leave till the Christmas 1958.

I found my last six-week school holidays very lonely, as this was the first time in my young life that I had no friends to be with, day after day I struggled to think of things to do on my own. I still had three months of schooling left to do and my friends were at work and no longer interested in playing out in the evenings in the street. They were now young working adults. Being on my own for those last three months after being with my friends from the age of five and doing so many things together, I found very traumatic.

I still wanted to play, but day after day I was alone. I went to the park just like I did with my friends, sat by the river, and went cycling to the places we all went. I wanted to play football just like I had done for so many years but I had no friends to play games with anymore. It wasn't the same now, I was lonely and lost with only the memories of the things we all did together. Even running errands lost its magic. My friends now just wanted to act like grown-ups.

It's a shame to lose one's childhood overnight and when one leaves school that's exactly what happens.

Christmas 1958 finally arrived and I left school, I was now classed as a working man. So now I became a lodger expected to pay my way in life, that was the hardest step in life I think that I ever had to take, the transition from boy to man.

103. SLANG PHRASES

£1 (a nicka, a sheet, a quid, one pound, a wonna) – 240 pennies
10/- (half a sheet, ten bob, half a nicka, ten shillings) – 120 pennies
5/- (a dolla, 5 bob, 5 shillings) – 60 pennies
2/6d (half a dolla, 2 and a kick, 2 shillings and sixpence) – 30 pennies
2/- (2 bob, 2 shillings) – 24 pennies
1/- (a bob, one shilling) – 12 pennies
6d (a tanna) – six pennies
Ain't – not doing it, not going
Nunk – nothing
Wunt – won't do it – won't have anything to do with it
Nowt – nothing
Safta – this afternoon
Gooin – going
Yo – you
Tat – scrap metal
Tatin – collecting metal rubbish
Pics – cinema, pictures, flicks
Fleapit – cinema
Got no coppa – got no pennies
Not a farthing – stony broke
No brass – no money
Broke – no money
No spondulaks – no money
No akkers – no money
My tart – my girl, nice girl
Tart – lady of the night
Old girl – mother
Old man – father or dad

Sis – sister
Bro – brother
Wick – week
Kissa – face
Straighten your kissa – stop pulling faces
Gob – mouth
Gob smacked – shocked
Cut – river or canal

We children grew up talking like this. At times I still do without realising I am saying it.

APPENDIX

by Trevor's son, Paul

It brings back a lot of memories, some good, but also emotional after losing my dad to Covid. He lived his life as he wanted and told me a lot of stories about the things he did as a youngster and growing up. My dad and David Prosser were close friends from toddlers to the day he left us. The things they did were helpful, they enjoyed doing little jobs for people especially the elderly, things today children would never think of doing. Their upbringing wasn't good, but they were loved. They were poor but approached everything with determination. My love for my dad will always be with me, he never took life too seriously, but I believe he was one of the best car salesmen in Birmingham.

I miss his smile and his funny ways, I think a lot of my dad's sense of humour was passed down to me and I am proud to be like him, humble, caring, funny and living for the day. Reading David Prosser's book makes me smile, sometimes laugh, but also emotional, as I loved my dad more than anything.

Thank you David, for keeping my dad's memory alive in this book. He may be gone but he could never be forgotten, as my dad would say every day to us.

Goodnight, God Bless, I Love You.
Rest in Peace Dad,
Your forever loving son, Paul.

Trevor (left) and me (right).
Lifelong friends from the age of four, reminiscing about our childhood.